PURPOSES OF THE AMERICAN ALLIANCE FOR HEALTH, PHYSICAL EDUCATION, RECREATION AND DANCE

The American Alliance is an educational organization, structured for the purposes of supporting, encouraging, and providing assistance to member groups and their personnel throughout the nation as they seek to initiate, develop, and conduct programs in health, leisure, and movement-related activities for the enrichment of human life.

Alliance objectives include:

1. Professional growth and development--to support, encourage, and provide guidance in the development and conduct of programs in health, leisure, and movement-related activities which are based on the needs, interests, and inherent capacities of the individual in today's society.

2. Communication--to facilitate public and professional understanding and appreciation of the importance and value of health, leisure, and movement-related activities as they contribute toward human well-being.

3. Research--to encourage and facilitate research which will enrich the depth and scope of health, leisure, and movement-related activities, and to disseminate the findings to the profession and other interested and concerned publics.

4. Standards and guidelines--to further the continuous development and evaluation of standards within the profession for personnel and programs in health, leisure, and movement-related activities.

5. Public affairs--to coordinate and administer a planned program of professional, public, and governmental relations that will improve education in areas of health, leisure, and movement-related activities.

6. To conduct such other activities as shall be approved by the Board of Governors and the Alliance Assembly, provided that the Alliance shall not engage in any activity which would be inconsistent with the status of an educational and charitable organization as defined in Section 501 (c)(3) of the Internal Revenue Code of 1954 or any successor provision thereto, and none of the said purposes shall at any time be deemed or construed to be purposes other than the public benefit purposes and objectives consistent with such educational and charitable status.

Bylaws, Article III

Preface

This book is intended to serve as a resource and stimulant for professionals involved in recreational and educational programs serving elementary-school-age learners. Experienced administrators and programmers of recreational services, whether those services are sponsored by a municipality, youth service agency, church, or the military, are in constant search of fun learning activities which will enrich their current program. Good educators are looking for unique educational approaches to add to their lessons. Others recognize the increased time demands placed on the school and realize the shrinking amount of time afforded to movement--particularly outdoors. The ideas in this book are intended for all those professionals.

The book is also intended to stimulate those who find themselves in a programming and professional rut. The proverbial physical educators who are tempted to roll out the balls and then blow the whistle at the end of the period may find the activities herein to be usable in their classes. The recreation professional who has sponsored the same program for the last 20 years with declining attendance may find some of the book's contents useful.

The authors have attempted to write in a style which the reader will find "user friendly." Attempts at humor and use of metaphor are intended to keep the text informal and enjoyable.

The thoughts concerning facilitation and the listed activities are not claimed by the authors to be original We extend appreciation to the originators and other authors who have recorded similar approaches and activities in their writings. The methods of facilitation and activities contained in the book are ones which the authors have used successfully or have observed being used with much success.

The activities work well with elementary-school-age children, adolescents, and adults. The setting for the activities is in the out-of-doors. This location is often overlooked as a teaching/learning/ activity station in favor of a more controllable artificial environment. The authors encourage you not to be one who overlooks the benefits offered by the outdoors. Even if you read no further in this book, consider getting your group outdoors! Instead of three straight weeks of tumbling during the winter term, have a day of ice skating on the local pond. Instead of another softball game, pull a couple of interested kids aside and offer them the opportunity to learn to fly cast. Take abstract concepts of math and show how they can be applied to answer questions and solve problems out-of-doors.

Please read the chapters concerning "How to Use This Book" and "The Art of Being an Effective Facilitator" prior to reading and employing the activities.

Contents

CHAPTER 5

CHAPTER 6

Chapter 1

How to Use This Book

Read it! Think about it! Use the good material, improve the mediocre to meet your needs, and pass over the unusable. Hopefully there are some of the 40 activities which you can use as presented herein. You will more than likely need to make adjustments to most of the activities to fit your situation and you are encouraged to do so. The activity descriptions are generic at best. Take an idea and make it bigger, smaller, or twist it a bit. Make it work for you!

Activity Selection

The activities selected by the authors are representative of those that could be used in a variety of settings for many types of groups.

The goals and objectives of your sponsoring organization and the expectancies of the administration are significant forces in the selection of appropriate activities. You as the facilitator of the activity are a force with goals, objectives, expectancies, and skills. The groups you are working with have their own skills, needs, and desires. The fourth force is a combination of available resources including time, funds, weather, and personnel. These forces are not constant and you, therefore, must monitor the pressure of all forces in order for the best activity to be selected for the right group at the right time and with the given available resources (see Chart 1).

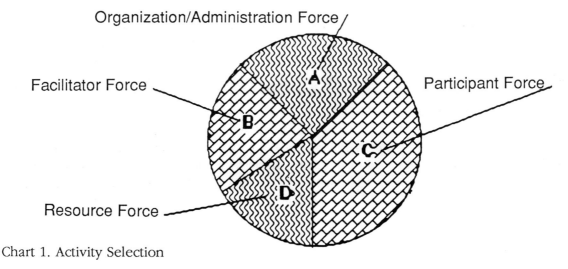

Chart 1. Activity Selection

Imagine the circle in Chart 1 in three dimensions as an inflatable beachball. Each chamber (A, B, C, and D) has an independent valve which allows a measured volume of "air" to be admitted. Each chamber has force and exerts pressure on the surface of the ball (the total activity situation) and on the internal baffles which separate the compartments and yet provide structural integrity. The needs of the participants (C) can exert enough force so that that chamber becomes the dominant force in selection of an activity. Time as a factor in chamber D can dominate as can the presence or absence of facilitator skill in chamber B. The point is that the facilitator must recognize the forces and the pressures exerted in order to select an activity from the book which will best serve all involved.

Additional Criteria for Selecting Activities

You as the facilitator must know that the activity is safe for the participants, yourself, and all other personnel involved. When using outdoor experiential activities you cannot guarantee that the group or individuals within the group will be "safe" from physical or emotional harm. But when can you? Outdoor activities can be as safe or safer than indoor activities. Do not let the issue of safety be an excuse to not use outdoor experiential activities.

The facilitator should be able to provide the appropriate equipment and learning aids to make the activity a success. The logistics, as well, must be feasible. The activities described beginning in Chapter 3 require minimal props or supplies and can be facilitated in almost any outdoor environment.

The activities you select should be socially acceptable. An activity such as "The Decreasing Square" (getting a group into a smaller and smaller area) described in Chapter 3 would meet this criteria. If the participants were nude, however, the social acceptability might be questioned by those you serve in certain communities in our nation.

Select activities which will not harm the natural environment. Your presence in that environment will have an impact on it. That impact, however, can be minimal if you use common sense, a respect for the environment, and conscientious selection of the activity to take place in that environment.

Select activities which have and can be justified by traditional educational and recreational values. Ask yourself, "Will this activity help the participants appreciate nature, beauty, art, literature, science, themselves, and/or others? Will the activity assist the participant in being able to think critically, solve problems, and communicate effectively? Is it fun? Is it healthy?" The activities described in this book will, hopefully, receive positive responses from its readers to at least one of those questions.

The maturity (not necessarily chronological age), ability, knowledge, and skill of the participant must be considered when selecting an activity and/or modifying that activity. People who lack any of these in relation to an activity in which they are asked to participate will experience frustration, anger, and resentment. If this is a goal of the facilitator, giving the group something they are not ready for is the way to achieve that goal. On the other hand, boredom and disinterest are the results experienced when a group is "beyond" an activity.

Activities for Special Groups

The activities described in this book are purposefully generic; modifications for special groups and special individuals have not been included. This is not because of lack of awareness or sensitivity. It is because the situation each facilitator will face with unique individuals in varied settings will require case-by-case modifications. Look at the described activity and the group or individual of your concern and adjust the procedure, materials, time requirement, etc.

Two reminders on working with special populations are important when facilitating outdoor experiential activities:

> 1. Ask the individual or group what would work best for them. They have lived with and known themselves longer than you have.

> 2. Provide the least restrictive activity environment. For some this may mean selecting a special activity site so they can participate from a wheelchair. For another, the provision of special activity locations, materials, or equipment would be viewed by that individual as restrictive. How do you know? Refer to reminder one.

Multiple Goal Activities

As you use this book, recognize that most of the activities have more than one goal or objective. In many cases, what would seem to be the obvious goal to an outsider observing the activity is in reality only a minor or even insignificant goal. John Dewey, the pragmatic American philosopher, refers to this in *Experience and Education* as "collateral learning."

> Collateral learning in the way of formation of enduring attitudes, of likes and dislikes, may be and often is much more important than the spelling lesson or lesson in geography or history that is learned. For these attitudes are fundamentally what count in the future. The most important attitude that can be formed is that of desire to go on learning.

Willi Unsoeld, the mountaineer and professor, spoke of the "Split Vision Theory of Education" during a presentation at an Association of Experiential Education Conference. He asked that you visualize walking a trail at night. When you look directly at the trail it is hard to see. Focusing to the side of the path allows you to see where you want to go. Education may be the same. If you focus on the goal, you may miss it. Focus on an adjacent area and the goal is easier to attain.

As you use the activities in this book, you will find one titled "Fire Building Problem." The building of the fire and boiling of the water and even the winning of the competition are important goals. They are obvious and recognized by the participants. In addition and more importantly, the facilitator recognizes the multiple activity goals that include group problem solving, organization of materials, lessons in division of labor, and effective communication.

Likewise, many of the activities that have a focus on problem solving in a specific "academic" area involve physical movement. The thoughtful facilitator can attack some physical fitness goals without the group thinking about the exercise. The authors suggest that facilitators be familiar with AAHPERD's Physical Best and Feelin' Good programs, making use of the Instructor's Guide to Physical Best and the Educational Packages (available from AAHPERD, 1900 Association Drive, Reston, VA 22091).

Activity Modes

The mode in which an activity should best be presented is not completely described in this book's activity descriptions. The facilitator, again, must consider the forces of the activity situation and present the activity in the appropriate mode. Is it best that activity X be presented didactically, via exploratory learning, be adventuresome, or take on elements of the stress/challenge mode?

Didactic Mode—The key feature of this mode is instruction from the teacher to the student. The method is expository. The teacher explains how to do something. The advantages of this method include teacher control of the order and pace of teaching and completion of the teaching in a relatively short period of time. The disadvantage, in the most extreme didactic situation, is that the teacher presents the activity and its associated information without regard to the differences in groups, individuals, and types of teaching stations.

Exploratory Learning Mode—This mode places the activity focus on the participant and learning as opposed to the focus being on the teacher and teaching. The proponents of this mode claim that the learning that takes place is enduring because learners want to learn and take ownership of the discoveries they have made during their exploration. Critics point out that all participants will not be ready to learn at the same time. The questions and reflected concerns of the participants may vary in direction. The facilitator, therefore, must plan more time for the activity and work with smaller groups of participants. This mode takes more time and the facilitator does not know what direction the learning will take. In the most extreme case, the idea of "learning what you want, when you want, or when you have a need to learn it" describes the mode.

4

Adventure Mode—The concept of being unsure of the outcome (risk) is inherent in the adventure mode. To assist in creating risk, the activity should be new to the participants and take place in an unfamiliar environment. This is an integral concept which allows "adventure courses" or "ropes courses" to be successful. The participants know they can walk 10 feet on a 24-inch diameter log and not fall off—when it is on the ground. But when it is suspended from a cable at each end so that it moves, or they are asked to walk backwards on a log at 40 feet above the ground, risk is introduced. They are unsure of their physical ability to accomplish the task. They are unsure of how they are going to feel while attempting the task. It is an adventure. Take note that adventure activities should also be fun and that participation should be voluntary.

Stress/Challenge Mode—The stress/challenge mode is similar to the adventure mode with the exception of the fun and voluntary criteria. This is a valid mode for some delivery systems or when utilized with specific individuals.

The activities included in this book can be presented in a manner which fits any or all of the modes mentioned. In reality, the facilitator will use the modes in combination. There will need to be some explanation (didactic) to provide basic activity conduct information and skills required for activity participation. Exploratory learning will also take place. The level of physical, affective, and/or cognitive risk associated with any of the activities can be managed. The elements of stress and challenge can be prescribed. The mixture and degree of each that will occur is something that the facilitator can orchestrate.

Use the book as the seed of an idea for an activity. Facilitators must nourish, prune, and pamper the activity with their skills and knowledge in order for the participant to harvest maximum benefits.

Selected Terminology

The authors have used the term "facilitator" for two reasons. The first is to encourage an attitude and approach to the described activities which they believe assists in the intended experiential learning. Second, facilitator is meant to include classroom teachers, program leaders, unit directors, camp counselors, scout masters, recreation coordinators, and any others who have responsibility for learners and opportunity to make learning easier.

The term "participant" includes students, campers, scouts, and other learners of all ages housed in a variety of activity delivery systems, such as recreation departments, public schools, youth organizations, etc.

Activity Description Format

Following the chapter on "The Art of Being an Effective Facilitator," the book is divided into four chapters with titles indicating the type of activities to be found therein.

Each activity has a title. In some cases, the title is descriptive of the activity, either to help the reader identify the activity or because the authors lacked the ability to be more creative. For other activities, the titles are ambiguous and the general description must be investigated in order to determine the nature of the activity.

The general description and objective(s) section for each activity provides a verbal sketch explaining the purpose, organization, and implementation of the specific activity. The reader must recognize the generic approach utilized and begin to make marginal notes for modifications for a specific situation.

In some activity descriptions, special skills needed for participation are referenced. No special skills are needed for most of the activities. The intent, however, is for this section to serve as a reminder to the facilitator to think about the psychomotor, affective, and cognitive skills appropriate for participation.

The references to group size and number of facilitators are based on what the authors see as realistic as opposed to ideal. The facilitator/participant ratio is an important consideration in terms of safety and maximum educational benefit. Facilitators of outdoor experiential activities should be sure to operate with facilitator/participant ratios falling within the guidelines suggested by national organizations associated with particular types of activities. As an example, refer to the Association for Experiential Education's Accepted Peer Practices in Adventure Programming, the American Red Cross for activities associated with waterfront activities, or the American Canoe Association for canoeing related experiences.

The section of the activity descriptions referring to age group suggests a minimal chronological age for participation. Level of maturity is what the facilitator should be thinking about. A ten-year-old with the math skills of a fifteen-year-old may be able to participate in math-associated activities beyond the chronological age. A sixteen-year-old with the psychomotor ability of a nine-year-old will have difficulties participating in a physical activity suggested for a participant of at least ten years of age.

Where needed, the safety and environmental considerations have been included. Sections have also been included concerning the facility and equipment needs and average time requirements.

Chapter 2

The Art of Being an Effective Facilitator

Facilitation of outdoor experiential learning activities is an art, for which the artist's tools are ideas for fun and learning in the form of activities that take place in a supportive environment. The medium is not stone, wood, or clay; the medium is the participants who are involved in activities. The responsibility of the facilitator (the artist) to the participants (the medium) is a serious one. For if the medium is damaged, people can not just be tossed aside nor can they be melted down for another project. To be an effective and responsible facilitator there are at least ten viable principles that should be considered.

Principle One: Why?

The effective facilitator must ask these questions. "Why am I going to facilitate this activity?" "What are my reasons?" "Is it the best educational and/or recreational experience to satisfy those reasons?" "Where will the activity lead?"

The basic thesis stated by L. B. Sharp, an icon in the history of outdoor education, applies: "That which can best be learned inside the classroom should be learned there. That which can best be learned in the out-of-doors through direct experience, dealing with native materials and life situations, should there be learned."

To facilitate an activity to fill time is not enough. To facilitate an activity without justification or a rationale is prostitution of the education and recreation professions.

Principle Two: Focus on the Participant

The artist's mediums of music, theater, or paint result in an end product which can be viewed, appreciated, and critiqued by others. Concerts, plays, and paintings are the result of the artist's work which receive such attention. Attention to the artist is through the product. While many of us can recognize "The William Tell Overture," we usually tend to think of the

Lone Ranger instead of the composer. The same applies to experiential activities The spotlight must be on the participant and not the facilitator. It is the participant who must have an enjoyable experience and learn. This is not to say that facilitators should not have fun in their work or that they will not learn from experience. Quite the opposite will most likely prove to be the case.

Experiential activities should satisfy the participants' needs and involve them fully. *The facilitator positively manipulates the activity environment for the benefit of the participant. It is the activity environment that "leads" and "teaches," not the facilitator.*

Principle Three: Encourage Exploratory Learning

Outdoor experiential activities offer opportunities for a participant to discover a method that works or a solution to a problem. *A "discovery" will be valued and remembered by participants because they did it; they were not told how to do it.*

As an example, *teaching* a group to find north without the use of a compass but by using the "stick and shadow" or "watch" methods is a fairly easy task for the teacher. In some cases, all that needs to be done is to share illustrations of the methods. A step-by-step presentation with demonstration will take little time and will yield a group who can repeat the task. There is structure, an allotted time period, and the teacher is in control. Being assured that the participants understand and remember the process is another matter.

Facilitating the activity may amount to an initial question, "How can we use the sun, a stick, and a watch to find north?" This is where the fun begins for the facilitator, who does not know what the responses will be. This is where the learning begins for the participants because they have to think. "Can it be done? What relationship is there between time, the sun, and direction?" Maybe someone in the group knows the answer. Great! The opportunity now exists for them to give an explanation and demonstration. Others in the group can doubt, question, and test their understanding. Maybe the group has no idea of where to start. They probably, however, have more knowledge than they realize and the facilitator's role is to guide to discovery. The temptation is to show and tell! Fight the temptation for the benefit of the participant. When the concept clicks and the mental light bulb flashes, you will see a sparkle in their eyes.

Principle Four: Create a "Need to Know"

An effective facilitator designs situations which encourage the participant to want to learn. For instance, teaching canoe strokes without the opportunity to go on a canoe trip can produce mediocre performance on the part of the participants. They ask, "Why are we doing this?" On the other hand, designing a situation where the group is on one side of the lake and their dinner is on the other side creates a "need to know" situation. The participants want to learn and have an opportunity to use the newly acquired skill. They watch, experiment, listen, try—and learn. They have a need to know.

Principle Five: Use the Teachable Moment

"It is Tuesday, so it must be Rome." "We saw 25 countries in five days." That has to be a horrible way to travel. The photographs which come from that type of trip are 80 percent self-portrait reflections off the inside of the bus window. This is a good indication that the traveler saw something interesting but was not allowed to get a closer look.

In education and recreation we must be careful not to take a similar trip. Sure, we need some structure to avoid chaos. Blindly worshiping a schedule, however, to the detriment of the participant's needs is negligent. On a hike through the woods, you may have a plant identification objective. Your group discovers a variety of animal tracks. "What are these? How big was it? Which way was it going?" This is the teachable moment. They want to learn. They are interested. It can be an ideal moment for the recreation and education professional. If you are stiff and only prepared to deal with plants, you'll miss the teachable moment and lose the group. If you are an effective facilitator, the unforeseeable teachable moment will provide an enriching experience. You don't even need to know the answers to their questions. You can help by asking your own questions and pointing the group toward methods and resources which will answer their questions.

Principle Six: Use Progressions

Work from the simple to the complex. Use each activity as a building block for the next. Activities which incorporate the use of topographical maps should not be presented until the participants have a basic understanding of the use of a compass and some experience with time and distance estimations. The effective facilitator will be prepared to use the map for the activity. In addition, the facilitator must be prepared to provide experiences concerning how the map was made and how the participants might use a map in the future. Be careful not to violate Principle Five when implementing Principle Six.

Principle Seven: Allow Failure

The effective facilitator must expect to observe, accept, and utilize participant failure as well as success. This principle goes hand-in-hand with discovery learning. Participants must discover what works and what does not. They must be allowed to live with and adjust to their mistakes.

This principle does not mean that the facilitator sets the group up for failure or suggest that the facilitator would allow the participant to become physically or emotionally endangered. There is an obvious responsibility to facilitate safe activities and provide protection for the participants. There are, however, safe mistakes and failures which can enrich experiential learning. Allow a group to walk in the wrong direction for a few miles. They will remember. Allow them to continue to work on a cardboard boat that will obviously sink. They need to experience the results.

Principle Eight: Do Not Abuse or Misuse the Tools

The master carpenter maintains a set of tools. Some of those tools are used every working day. Other tools are always in the tool box but only used for brief moments for a special purpose. If one does not have the right tool for the job at hand, several consequences are experienced. One, the job cannot be completed. Two, a substitute tool can be improvised, but that usually takes valuable time while the job waits. Three, the wrong tool is used and the job is botched.

If one has all of the right tools but not the skills and knowledge to use those tools, problems can occur. One, the tool can be damaged to the point of being useless. Two, the medium on which the tool was applied can be damaged.

The effective facilitator has a full tool chest and the knowledge and skill to use all of the tools. The facilitator uses a screwdriver on screws and a well sharpened carving tool on a sculpture—not vice versa.

Principle Nine: Leave Them High

The effective facilitator must have a sense of timing. An activity should be taken to the apex and terminated. This requires the facilitator to sense participant interest, degree of involvement, and "stamina" in relation to time.

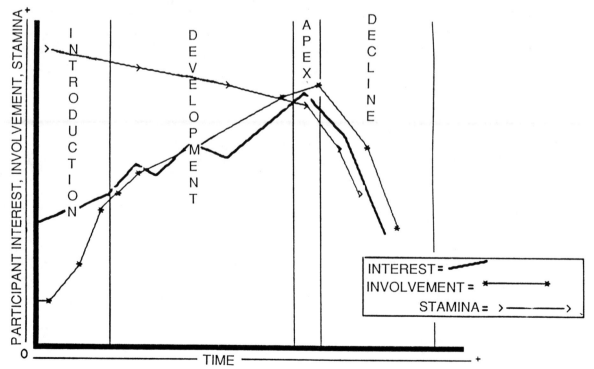

We assume that participants enter the activity with some degree of interest and stamina (although there are times when this is not the case). Their interest and involvement should increase during the introduction and developmental stages. At some point in time they are going to "top out." Their stamina is reaching a limit and their interest and involvement have peaked. This is the moment to terminate the activity. If you go too far and too long, it is a rapid descent to low interest and declining involvement. You have lost them. You will hear, "The activity was okay but I don't want to do it again." If, however, you quit at the right time, you have a satisfied group. Or if the group is upset with you as the facilitator, it is because they wanted to do more. You did not give them enough. They want to come back and do it again. Ah! You got them. They are excited about the activity and want to continue.

Principle Ten: Review, Analyze, Summarize, and Project

John Dewey used the term "reconstruction." Psychologists use "processing" and "feedback." The military "debriefs."

The terminology the facilitator uses is not of importance. The act of reviewing, analyzing, and summarizing an experience is an essential element of experiential learning. Think about it a minute. When do you learn? Do you learn while the action is taking place? Sure, a portion of the learning takes place then. But, it is only after one is able to see the results of that action and reflect on the action that led to the results that one has significant learning. Learners must also project their newly acquired information into the future in terms of planning similar action or modifying their former action.

The beginning backcountry skier out on an overnight trip for the first time with a heavy pack will most likely have a series of experiential learning moments. There will come the time when both ski tips engage themselves in deep snow or pierce a slight dip while the skier is moving rapidly downhill. The skier soon finds his or her head planted in that deep snow between the ski tips. In about seven tenths of a second, that heavy pack follows and grinds the head a bit deeper into the snow. The skier tries to get up. Skis, poles, pack, and body parts are entangled. It's a fight! Just as the sweaty skier rises, the pack shifts, the skis slip, and the skier ends up on his/her back feeling like an inverted turtle.

What has the skier learned at this moment? Very little. It is only when the action which led to the less than desirable results is reviewed, analyzed, and summarized that significant learning takes place. "I was going too fast. I did not recognize the change in snow surface. Both feet were together and not in a wider base that a telemark position would have provided. It might have been easier to take the pack off before trying to get up." This information is now projected into future actions.

The effective facilitator can assist in this step of experiential learning. Take time to review, analyze, summarize, and project. This principle is often violated leaving the learner hanging.

Other Considerations

Contagion—Be aware of the rapid spread of feelings. When the facilitator approaches the group with enthusiasm and confidence, the group will most often reciprocate. Likewise, if the facilitator is glum and believes the activity to be a joke, the group becomes contaminated and will reflect that attitude. Believe in what you are doing and approach the activity in a positive manner.

Nonintimate Touching—Many outdoor experiential activities demand a helping hand. The helping hand is often the facilitator assisting a participant. This assistance may be in the form of "spotting" a fall, lifting a person out of the water, checking a personal floatation device or a climbing harness. Just do it! If the facilitator does not make a big deal of holding a participant's hand or giving a helping push on the rear end, the group will not even notice. If the facilitator makes an issue of it, the group will make it an even bigger issue. Remember contagion. It applies here also. The effective facilitator will provide a model which allows nonintimate touching among the group to be comfortable.

Position—The outdoor experiential activities facilitator is not in front of the classroom or on the stage of the recreation center's activity room. These are artificial environments designed to focus attention on the teacher or leader. For experiential activity facilitation, the facilitator is in a natural environment and must place the participant in the comfortable position. The facilitator should face the sun, not the group. The group should be able to look down on the facilitator demonstrations and from the same direction as the facilitator. This may mean you need to get on your knees while the group looks over your shoulder. This consideration is often forgotten. It is sad to see a group of kids squinting into the sun and only being able to see the silhouette of what they are supposed to see.

Communication—Within your group, you have auditory learners, visual learners, and kinesthetic learners. Most, of course, combine these modes of learning. The point is that what the group hears should be a complete message. What they see should also be complete. Then they need an opportunity to do.

From the facilitator's perspective, you should coordinate what you are saying with what the group is seeing you do. If your verbal presentation is a step ahead of your visual presentation, expect group confusion. Test this thought with a knot tying or a map and compass session.

Chapter 3

Teamwork Activities

ACTIVITY TITLE: Bomb Squad

GENERAL DESCRIPTION AND OBJECTIVE(S): The objective in this activity is to develop leadership, cooperation, and teamwork among the participants. While a knowledge of ropework, primarily the tripod or shear lashing, is definitely helpful, this activity can be accomplished without any formal training in that area.

The activity centers on the solving of a certain problem; a "bomb" has been placed in the area and the participants are asked to remove it. The bomb is a number-ten tin can with a bail attached and filled with colored water. The participants are instructed that the bomb, sitting on the ground, is being cooled rapidly by the earth's surface, and that:

1. The liquid will explode if it gets too cool.
2. It may explode if any of it splashes out.
3. It may explode if any noise or talking occurs within 10 feet of it.
4. It may explode if anyone touches the bucket.

Because the bomb is so sensitive, the participants must follow this procedure silently:

1. Make a tripod in order to get the bomb off the ground.
2. Hang the bomb from the tripod without touching the bomb itself.
3. Float a lighted candle on the liquid to keep it warm.
4. Using the tripod, three participants must carry the bomb 50 feet.
5. No spilling or dropping.
6. The candle may not go out longer than 15 seconds.
7. No talking within 10 feet.

Because of the seemingly complex nature of the task, the facilitator should give the participants some time to organize themselves and discuss how potential problems might be handled. The eventuality of the candle going out, for example, might call for a participant whose sole responsibility is to follow along with the tripod crew, match in hand, ready to strike it should the need arise. Also, the need for silence will call for some advance planning on the part of the participants.

VARIATIONS: Save the Whale
                     Ice Fishing Rig

SPECIAL SKILLS NEEDED FOR PARTICIPATION: None.

GROUP SIZE: Six to eight participants per group.

AGE GROUP: Twelve years and older.

NUMBER OF FACILITATORS: One facilitator for every two or three groups.

DESCRIPTION OF EQUIPMENT AND FACILITIES:

      1. An open area with a "safety zone" where the "bomb" is to be placed 50 feet from the original starting point.
      2. One "bomb" and floating candle holder with candle for each group. (Note: The can should be equipped with a handle so it can be suspended by rope without touching the can itself. A distinctive paint job on the can would dress it up, too.)
      3. Three eight-foot poles per group.
      4. Rope. (Note: For poles up to three inches in diameter, 1/4-inch rope seems to work well. For poles over three inches in diameter, 3/8-inch rope works better. Because the tripod has to be moved, it is strongly recommended that the smaller poles be used. In determining how much rope is needed, allow one yard of rope for each inch of the combined diameters of the poles. For example, if participants will be lashing three two-inch poles together, add the three diameters together [2 + 2 + 2 = 6]. Thus you will need six yards of rope for the lashing. Figuring an additional foot or two in order to suspend the bomb from the tripod, 20 feet of rope should cover the job.)

TIME REQUIREMENT: Twenty to 30 minutes.

ACTIVITY TITLE: Save the Whale

GENERAL DESCRIPTION AND OBJECTIVE(S): While many might look at finding the solution to the problem as the objective to this activity, the real objective is the development of team work within the group of participants. There can be several solutions to the problem. The problem is that the mouth of a harbor has been blocked by an ice flow and a gray whale has been trapped in the harbor. Since the whale is unable to make her migration to the southern breeding grounds, the participants need to open the mouth of the harbor in order to free her. Several weak spots in the ice have been selected for "dynamite" placement. Participants must plant the "dynamite." Since the blasting points are on very thin ice, it is necesary to stay at least 15 feet away from the various locations. The facilitator should mark 15-foot radius circles around the blasting points. The firing mechanism is very delicate, so participants cannot throw or drop the "dynamite." While this activity is natural for the snow, it can be accomplished any time of year in practically any location--even in a large building, such as a gymnasium, if necessary.

VARIATIONS: Bomb Squad and Ice Fishing Rig

SPECIAL SKILLS NEEDED FOR PARTICIPATION: None.

GROUP SIZE: Six to eight participants per group.

AGE GROUP: Twelve years and older.

NUMBER OF FACILITATORS: One for every two groups.

DESCRIPTION OF EQUIPMENT AND FACILITIES: This activity can take place almost anywhere. The area selected, though, should be fairly open and have plenty of room to mark the "blasting points."
    1. Four sticks of "dynamite" per group. These can be ten-inch sections of dowel or broom handle painted red.
    2. Four stakes in the ground to mark blasting points.
    3. Fifteen-foot string to mark circles around each blasting point scratched in ground.
    4. A collection of poles and ropes of various lengths. (Remember, there are many solutions. For example, poles could be lashed to 15-foot lengths, or ropes could be tied together with the "dynamite" in the middle and lowered into position from both sides.)

SAFETY AND ENVIRONMENTAL CONSIDERATIONS: While the hypothetical situation takes place on the ice, it is best that the actual activity does not.

TIME REQUIREMENT: This particular activity has the potential of going on for a long period of time as participants discuss possible solutions. In order to limit discussion and to keep enthusiasm high, it might be well to mention that the timing mechanism on the "dynamite" has been set for 15 minutes. Of course, the facilitator can vary the time limit depending on the maturity of the participants.

ACTIVITY TITLE: Ice Fishing Rig

GENERAL DESCRIPTION AND OBJECTIVE(S): This activity is definitely not just for winter. In fact, while the objective may appear to be that of constructing an ice fishing rig, the real objective is to foster ingenuity, creativity, and morale.

The facilitator explains that an ice fishing rig is often useful in snowy climes during the winter to secure food. During the early morning hours, the ice is usually thick enough to walk on, but the heat of the midday sun weakens it. As a result, a device needs to be constructed that will allow participants to fish a spot at least 30 feet away without walking back on the ice.

Participants should be instructed to do the following:

1. Invent and construct an ice fishing rig.
2. Rig up a fishing line to a spot at least 30 feet away.
3. Make a gadget that will signal participants when they get a strike.

While decision making and organization are more important in this exercise than the actual solution, it is always interesting to see the various rigs the participants construct. A typical solution might be a simple tripod with a fishing line across the top, or a wooden crate with a line and a spring mechanism to signal a strike. In order to foster such creativity, a wide variety of materials should be made available for construction.

VARIATIONS: Bomb Squad
Save the Whale

SPECIAL SKILLS NEEDED FOR PARTICIPATION: None.

GROUP SIZE: Six to eight participants per group.

AGE GROUP: Twelve and older.

NUMBER OF FACILITATORS: One for every three groups.

DESCRIPTION OF EQUIPMENT AND FACILITIES:

1. An area large enough to construct the fishing rigs.
2. A variety of materials with which to spark creativity. These materials could include six- to eight-foot poles for lashing, various lengths of rope, wooden crates, hammer and nails, etc.

TIME REQUIREMENT: Thirty minutes.

ACTIVITY TITLE: Invisible Leader

GENERAL DESCRIPTION AND OBJECTIVE(S): The objective in this activity is to help the participants recognize and value the significance of communication in daily activities. While many individuals rely on the designated leader to provide guidance and direction, this exercise conveniently removes the leader in order to allow the other participants to not only develop individual leadership skills, but also realize the importance of communicating effectively.

To begin, each group is asked to choose a group representative. The representatives are taken aside and presented with a written problem. The facilitator should inform the group representatives that they only have one minute to read and digest the information given. The problem can take many forms, but it is important that several objectives be listed in the written instructions in order for participants to realize the necessity of effective communication. One example that has been effective is as follows:

> Your group has just been transported to another planet. Inhabitants of this planet have asked you to show them what life is like on earth. All you have to show them is what you can make from building blocks. (Note: Other items can also be used successfully, such as Tinkertoys, poles, rope, etc.) Take the box of blocks and construct a model of an object we see almost every day.
>
> Some extra blocks are available from the facilitator, if you need them. You may take no more than four extra blocks.
>
> When you have finished, line up by height in a straight line.

Representatives are then asked to return the written instructions and go to their groups to relate the information. After two minutes, the group representatives are to return to the facilitator and group members are to follow the instructions given.

During this exercise, while the group members are attempting to complete the problem, they are to have no contact with their group representatives. While questions inevitably arise, group members are forced to handle these situations within the group by making decisions among themselves.

When the groups have completed the problem, the facilitator should ask a group member to state aloud the instructions given by his/her group representative. The facilitator should then read the original instructions.

Expect a breakdown in communications somewhere in the process, either between the group representatives and the facilitator or between the group representatives and the groups. This is not only anticipated but highly desirable. These breakdowns are an ideal "stepping stone" to a discussion in effective communications. Some points that should be emphasized are the importance of note taking while receiving instructions (both by the group representatives and the group members), the significance of verbal and nonverbal communication, and the effectiveness of good written communications. Emphasis should also be placed on asking questions, clarifying statements, and repeating or paraphrasing instructions.

Written problems can vary depending upon group size, ability, location, and situation. The important thing to realize is that the problems need to be complicated enough to make the importance of communicative skills evident, yet simple enough to hold interest and create the perception that basic "word of mouth" instructions are sufficient.

VARIATIONS: The Return of the Invisible Leader
Pony Express

SPECIAL SKILLS NEEDED FOR PARTICIPATION: None.

GROUP SIZE: Five to eight participants per group. Four to five groups are probably the maximum with which most facilitators would like to work.

AGE GROUP: Twelve years of age is about the minimum.

NUMBER OF FACILITATORS: One facilitator can usually handle this fairly well. Occasionally two can be used if one observes the group members working through the problem while the other instructs the group representatives as to what is taking place, i.e., communicative processes, decision making, etc.

DESCRIPTION OF EQUIPMENT AND FACILITIES: This activity can take place just about anywhere—in a large field, in a classroom, outdoors under the trees—anywhere there is enough room for the participants to break into separate groups.

The equipment needed is dependent on the problem selected. A wide variety of materials have been used in the past.

SAFETY AND ENVIRONMENTAL CONSIDERATIONS: A word of caution—while building blocks, Tinkertoys, and popsicle sticks have been successfully used with groups of all ages, large eight-foot poles could prove hazardous with some of the younger groups.

TIME REQUIREMENT: Including the follow-up instruction on effective communication and a discussion of what transpired, the activity will normally take about one hour.

ACTIVITY TITLE: The Return of the Invisible Leader

GENERAL DESCRIPTION AND OBJECTIVE(S): This activity is generally used as a follow-up to the Invisible Leader activity in order to solidify communication skills.

As in the Invisible Leader, the groups are asked to send one group representative forward. Each representative is then given a written problem different from the problem presented in the Invisible Leader. The representatives have one minute to read and digest the problem. It might be well to note that it is not necessary to have the same group representatives as were used in the Invisible Leader. In fact, it might even be preferable to have different representatives.

During this stage of communicative skills learning, participants should automatically be taking notes regarding the problem. If this does not happen, the facilitator might want to remind the group representatives of the Invisible Leader activity.

The problem presented in the Return of the Invisible Leader should be more complicated than the Invisible Leader problem. Seemingly trivial instructions might even be included such as, "After one person in your group puts a block in place, he or she may not add another block until everyone else in the group has had a turn."

Representatives will return the instruction sheets to the facilitator and go to their respective groups to relate the information given. After two minutes, representatives will return to the facilitator and the group members will follow the instructions given.

When the groups have completed the problem and are standing or sitting in the positions they thought were requested, the facilitator should ask one of the members to repeat the instructions given by his or her group representative. The facilitator should then read the original instructions.

A discussion can follow comparing the results of the Invisible Leader with those of the Return of the Invisible Leader. If the results of the two activities were different, what made them different?

VARIATIONS: The Invisible Leader
Pony Express

SPECIAL SKILLS NEEDED FOR PARTICIPATION: None.

GROUP SIZE: Five to eight participants per group. Four to five groups will probably be the maximum one would want to have in this type of activity.

AGE GROUP: Twelve years old and above.

NUMBER OF FACILITATORS: One is usually sufficient.

DESCRIPTION OF EQUIPMENT AND FACILITIES: This type of activity can be done virtually anyplace where there is enough room for the participants to separate into groups.

The equipment is dependent upon what type of problem is selected. Note taking supplies should be available.

SAFETY AND ENVIRONMENTAL CONSIDERATIONS: Same as for the Invisible Leader.

TIME REQUIREMENT: If the participants have applied the communicative skills learned in the Invisible Leader activity, this activity should take considerably less time, unless the problem would require some extensive work, such as building a suspension bridge with large poles and rope. Normally, the exercise can be a successful tool in demonstrating how effective communications can be significant in the accomplishment of group goals.

ACTIVITY TITLE: Decreasing Square

GENERAL DESCRIPTION AND OBJECTIVE(S): Scribe a 20' square in the dirt. The group must stand inside the boundaries. A group of 12 to 15 will have no problems doing this. In fact, they can accomplish this without even touching each other—and they probably will not. Have them back out of the square. Now "cut the square in half." Have the group get inside the 10' x 20' rectangle. No problems here, but they are having to stand a bit closer or even touch each other. Now the "square" is decreased to 10' x 10', then 5' x 10', then 5' x 5', etc. At some point, depending on the size of the group and the size of the individuals in the group, they will have to mutually organize a method of holding on to each other and even climb on each other in order to have the entire group within the "square."

The surface objective of being able to accomplish the task is of little importance. Getting folks to touch each other (hold hands, push on backs, etc.) during the process is important. This "nonintimate" touching is important to establish within a group especially if the group is going to be involved in further outdoor activities together. Being comfortable with extending a helping hand to another to assist in climbing over a rough section of trail is important. Being okay to push on someone's rear end to get them on a horse is important.

Another objective this activity can accomplish concerns group cooperation and consideration. They will have to communicate in some form. They will have to depend on each other. One individual letting the rest of the group know what they can do to help the situation or that a hand is losing strength has transference to other group experiences.

This activity also gives the facilitator an opportunity to observe the group under controlled conditions. How do they work together? Who seems to be the leader(s)? Who does not contribute to the cause? Who is getting frustrated? Who is creative? These observations can assist in planning future activities as well as give the facilitator a "head start" on learning about the group.

VARIATIONS:

1. Select a leader who will direct all actions of the group from an external position. The group will only be able to do what the leader directs.
2. Select a leader who directs all actions and is also a group participant.
3. Blindfold the group.
4. Do not allow the group to talk.
5. Use a "circle of rope" that the entire group must stand "inside of" and lift the rope over their heads.
6. The Human Knot exercise from *Cowtails and Cobras* (edited by Karl Rohnke, and published in 1977 by Project Adventure, Inc., 775 Bay Road, Hamilton, MA 001936).

SPECIAL SKILLS NEEDED FOR PARTICIPATION: None.

GROUP SIZE: Twelve to fifteen.

AGE GROUP: Seven and older.

NUMBER OF FACILITATORS: One.

DESCRIPTION OF EQUIPMENT AND FACILITIES: Flat field.

SAFETY AND ENVIRONMENTAL CONSIDERATIONS:

1. Do not allow the participants to "stack" higher than on top of another's shoulders.
2. Watch for wrists being twisted and clothes being tugged on too hard.
3. If the group begins to climb on each other's back and/or shoulders, "spot" the group, to avoid problems.

TIME REQUIREMENT: Fifteen to twenty minutes.

ACTIVITY TITLE: Fire Building Problem

GENERAL DESCRIPTION AND OBJECTIVE(S): The obvious objective is to allow participants to gain skills in building a fire for use as an outdoor cooking and warming tool. Less obvious, yet as important, are skills in organization, group cooperation, and effective communication. In order for the group to be successful, materials must be gathered, duties assigned, and a strategy developed. All of these skills have carryover potential.

The process is for a group to gather fuel, lay a fire, light the fire, and have enough energy generated by that fire to burn a suspended string or boil a pot of water. The "string" method requires the facilitator or participants to place a string parallel to the ground 16 to 20 inches above the base of the fire. This is an easy system to set up but has a primary weakness. If the problem is to start a fire hot enough to burn the string, some literal and creative young mind might just light a match and burn the string. The problem is solved but your objectives have not been met.

Boiling a pot of water is a preferable method. It requires a sustained fire, adequate fuel supply, a water source, and a method of holding the pot above the fire. This system allows the group to realize a variety of chores to be accomplished and strategies to be developed and modified for success or failure to occur.

The creative facilitator will consider some embellishments to this activity. An example is to freeze messages in ice cubes. The ice cube is then melted in the hot water with the message directing the participants as to their next activity. Liquid soap added to the pot of water by the facilitator helps all to recognize when the water reaches a "good boil."

Some common problems you can anticipate are:

1. Everyone in the group gathers wood with no one getting water or beginning to prepare the fire.
2. The group gets a good fire going without having developed a method for holding the pot over the fire. The fire then dies as a method of "pot holding" is discovered and implemented and then more wood needs to be gathered.
3. Carelessness or a poor "pot holding" method allows the pot to tip and put out the fire.

This can be an activity with competition among the groups, a restrictive time limit, or both. While there is competition, there is also the need for group cooperation. This is an excellent activity in preparation for a camping trip where the group will be cooking for themselves. Camp chores require some thinking, planning, and coooperation.

VARIATIONS: Build a Shelter
Build a Boat

SPECIAL SKILLS NEEDED FOR PARTICIPATION: None.

GROUP SIZE: Three to five participants per group. Five groups will keep one facilitator busy.

AGE GROUP: Your judgment—old enough to be dealing with fire.

NUMBER OF FACILITATORS: The activity can be facilitated by one if the location allows that facilitator to keep tabs on all participants. If, however, the water source is a stream out of sight and 200 yards away and individuals are gathering fuel from throughout more than an acre of wooded land, additional assistance would be comforting.

DESCRIPTION OF EQUIPMENT AND FACILITIES:

1. Five wood stove matches per group.
2. One "number-ten" can per group (with bailing wire for a handle). The school cafeteria or restaurants have an ample supply of these.
3. A water supply—hose, well, stream, pond, etc.
4. Fuel supply—a wooded area or a box of kindling.
5. Shovel(s).
6. Fire extinguisher.
7. First aid kit.
8. One "fire pan" per group.

SAFETY AND ENVIRONMENTAL CONSIDERATIONS: Approval of appropriate officials is suggested. If you are in a rural area, a fire permit from the Forest Service, Bureau of Land Management, or the county may be required. An urban setting may require approval from the local fire department or fire marshal.

This activity provides the opportunity to invite officials to participate and may also serve as a lead-in activity to presentations related to fire that they may wish to provide.

If you are gathering fuel from a wooded area, have your groups gather only wood which is on the ground. Some limits on size of sticks should be mentioned or you may have logs being harvested by your adolescent timber fallers.

The fire areas should be located on a sandy or a gravel soil. If scarring of the area is a concern, you may want to use "fire pans." Metal trash can lids serve this purpose well. This is something you should supply. Asking your participants to bring this item may result in some neighborhood complaints.

Make certain that all fires are extinguished, using shovels or fire extinguishers as necessary.

TIME REQUIREMENT: Allow at least an hour for the activity and 15 to 20 minutes to discuss what happened. You may find a situation when the groups want to try again. If so, another 30 minutes will be required.

ACTIVITY TITLE: Build a Shelter

GENERAL DESCRIPTION AND OBJECTIVE(S): Shelter building is a very usable skill in the outdoors. This activity, therefore, has direct application as well as hosting an opportunity for problem solving and experience in group dynamics. The groups are to construct a shelter within a designated period of time. Natural resources can be used. Sticks, leaves, grass, and rocks can provide protection from the wind, rain, and sun. If you are in snow country, igloos, snow trenches, and snow caves become possible options. Ten by twelve plastic sheets with "parachute cord" are inexpensive and quite functional. The ultimate synthetic and mobile shelter is the backpacking tent. Just getting one of these set up in the dark for the first time can be an interesting problem.

This is a good lead-up activity for the outing you are planning for your group.

VARIATIONS: Fire Building Problem
Build a Boat

SPECIAL SKILLS NEEDED FOR PARTICIPATION: Variable. Information on site selection should be offered to the group either before, during, or after the activity.

When working with poles, logs, and sticks, some pre-activity instruction and practice with lashing would be appropriate. Tarp work requires methods of attaching line to the tarp, staking, and some basic knots. Snow shelter work requires a group that is outfitted well for the environment and has some proven skills in snow travel.

GROUP SIZE: Each group should consist of the number of people that the shelter will house.

AGE GROUP: Seven and older.

NUMBER OF FACILITATORS: One when the activity happens with a mature group of ten or less in good weather and when in reach of immediate outside assistance. With younger groups in a winter environment away from the trailhead, the facilitator/participant ratio must be adjusted.

DESCRIPTION OF EQUIPMENT AND FACILITIES: Variable.

SAFETY AND ENVIRONMENTAL CONSIDERATIONS: Be careful when using natural shelter materials. Manage the activity so that the area experiences minimum impact. Use only surface materials. Return those materials to where they were found at the completion of the exercise. Twenty youth from your organization armed with saws and axes could do heavy damage to an acre of land. You are not going to carry axes and saws into the backcountry; do not allow their use during this activity.

TIME REQUIREMENT: Variable. A 30-minute period may do for more mature groups using tents or tarps. A minimum of three hours will be required for a group of four digging a good snow cave which will sleep those four.

ACTIVITY TITLE: Build a Boat

GENERAL DESCRIPTION AND OBJECTIVE(S): Throughout the nation boating clubs sponsor various racing forms of "anything that floats except a boat." On Oregon's Rouge River, they use "Durt Bags." Mr. Durt encased foam packaging peanuts in a four-foot by eight-foot nylon net to create his craft, which is paddled by one or two enthusiasts. Ceramic toilets mounted on foam blocks have been seen in competition in southern Colorado's Rio Grande Raft Races, and sea kayaks built within an hour from scratch (paper, wood, plastic) form an annual regatta on San Francisco Bay.

This activity challenges the group to build a boat from cardboard, tape, and staples that will be capable of carrying one person a defined distance in open water. Group communication and cooperation are demanded for successful design and construction.

This is a fun activity which requires creative thinking and efficient use of limited resources. You can present the problem in a simple, straightforward way by giving each group identical resources (cardboard, tape, staples, knife). A more complex approach is to provide unequal resources. One group may have a surplus of cardboard and a staple gun but only five staples. Another group may have 200 staples, three feet of tape, and a lean supply of cardboard. This approach not only encourages cooperation within each group, but also among groups. The cooperation takes on an "edge" in that it is happening under an umbrella of competition. Each group wants to be the first to be successful. They realize they have resources others need and that others have resources they need. Negotiations are interesting and the "meat" of what you will discuss at the conclusion of the activity. Expect bartering to occur. Expect an outcry that the activity is unfair. Expect some laughs as the crafts attempt their voyage. Expect some clever designs that are successful on the water. Paddling by hand or by a cardboard paddle should be specified or determined optional.

VARIATIONS: Fire Building Problem
Build a Shelter

SPECIAL SKILLS NEEDED FOR PARTICIPATION:
1. Basic swimming ability for at least one person per group or a person who is water safe with the ability to wear a personal flotation device.
2. Safe use of a knife for cutting the cardboard.

GROUP SIZE: Two to five people per group. Five groups per session.

AGE GROUP: Ten years old is probably a minimum age.

NUMBER OF FACILITATORS: One.

DESCRIPTION OF EQUIPMENT AND FACILITIES:
1. A swimming pool, lake, pond, or slow moving river will work well.
2. Cardboard from bicycle or appliance boxes. Make sure to cut the bicycle boxes apart into some odd-shaped pieces. If you provide a whole box, it can simply be taped on the seams and floats quite well. You may want to force more effort than that process requires.
3. Knives or large scissors.
4. Packaging tape (duct, athletic, or masking tape will work but are not the best).
5. Staples and staplers.
6. Pencils.
7. Personal flotation devices (life jackets).
8. Rescue rope.
9. Wet suits for very cold water situations.
10. Camera (if you want to make a record of the creative results).

SAFETY AND ENVIRONMENTAL CONSIDERATIONS: The life jackets and wet suits are optional. You should use your best judgment concerning their use or nonuse. The rescue rope gives you an extended hand from the shore.

If you use a pool, make sure to retrieve all cardboard from the water. Even small, soaked pieces can cause problems for the filtering system. In a nonsynthetic body of water, make provisions for being able to dump the cardboard refuse. You might want to save it as a potential fuel source for the Fire Building Problem activity.

TIME REQUIREMENT: A minimum 90-minute time block.

Chapter 4

Outdoor Skill Acquisition Activities

ACTIVITY TITLE: Owls Eyes

GENERAL DESCRIPTION AND OBJECTIVE(S): Many young people, adolescents, and some adults have fears about being in the dark. Moving about in the outdoors during the night can produce additional anxiety. The purpose of this exercise is to provide some experience in night travel under controlled conditions.

To set up for this activity, the facilitator or more experienced participants place self-adhesive, reflective "eyes" on trees, rocks, buildings, or posts and pretest those placements. The placement is such that position "One" can be spotted from the starting point. Position "Two" can be spotted from position "One" and so forth. The participants, accompanied by a facilitator or group leader, begin at the appointed start and scan the area with a flashlight to find the "Owls Eyes." The group then carefully moves to position "One." The process is then repeated until completion.

It is important to get the group to employ all their senses. What do you hear? What do you smell? What do you feel with your feet? Spend some of the time moving with the flashlight ON. This provides opportunity for group cooperation and consideration of others. Spend some of the time with the flashlight OFF. This gives opportunity for development of night vision. After the eye adapts to the dark, there is, in most situations, adequate natural light for one to see and move about carefully. Explain the anatomy and physiology of the eye that allow for this adaptation. The participants may also notice that they can see better just off to the side than straight ahead. Experiment in the dark with looking right at the trail and looking just to the side of the trail.

VARIATIONS:

1. Messages or the components of a secret code can be affixed to each of the positions. A sponsor of a religious organization may elect to leave verses of scripture to be discussed. A group led by one with knowledge of the flora, fauna, and/or history of the area may want to incorporate that information into the messages. The physical educator can leave instructions for a specific type of physical exercise.

2. Additional sights and sounds can be added to those of natural origin. A pebble tossed or a bird call from a hidden facilitator can add some flavor to the experience. *Be careful to keep this approach under control.*

SPECIAL SKILLS NEEDED FOR PARTICIPATION: None.

GROUP SIZE: No more than five per group so that each individual has adequate opportunity to spot the "eyes" and operate the flashlight.

AGE GROUP: Seven years and older.

NUMBER OF FACILITATORS: One per group of five participants.

DESCRIPTION OF EQUIPMENT AND FACILITIES:
　　　1. One flashlight per group. Avoid having all participants in possession of flashlights. If each person has one, it takes away from the sense of group and a shared experience. It is also impossible to keep the lights switched off during times when you want to depend on night vision.
　　　2. This activity is best performed in a wooded area which is free from artificial light. Other locations will work with some thought and use of your imagination.

SAFETY AND ENVIRONMENTAL CONSIDERATIONS:
　　　1. The facilitators should carry an extra flashlight (hidden) in case of an emergency.
　　　2. All facilitators should have some common signal which aborts the activity and signifies the need for assistance.
　　　3. The area used should be free of artificial (broken glass, barbed wire fence, abandoned mine shafts) and natural (poison oak, swift moving water) hazards.

TIME REQUIREMENT: A minimum of one hour.

ACTIVITY TITLE: How to Get Lost

GENERAL DESCRIPTION AND OBJECTIVE(S): One of the concerns of managing a group in the outdoors is the potential for an individual, a couple, or an entire group becoming lost. The more your group understands about the process of being lost, the less likely they will actually become lost. If they do, that understanding will help them deal with the situation in a positive manner.

This activity is a series of two exercises which when completed will give the participant a better understanding of the "being lost" process. It is fun and educational. You may want to preface the activity by asking "Has anyone in the group been lost?" Be prepared for some interesting stories. The stories are usually not about themselves but a family member or a friend. You then want to explain that "being lost" is a matter of not knowing where you are in relation to the rest of the world. One's attitude in that situation can then be addressed. Point out the difference between panic and the thought that you are not "lost" but only "temporarily confused." Talk about the Indian who said, "Me not lost, tepee lost!"

The next step is to examine how one gets "lost." It boils down to losing track of time, distance, and direction. If we eliminate full functioning of one or more of our senses, our calculations concerning time, distance, and direction become less accurate. In this series of exercises the elimination of sight is the active ingredient.

Exercise 1 (Time): Split the groups into two sections. Have Group A either close their eyes or blindfold themselves. Ask each individual in Group A to raise their hands at time intervals of one, two, and three minutes after you give the signal to begin. At the conclusion of what they determine to be minute three, they can open their eyes or remove the blindfold and quietly join Group B. The individuals in Group B have the responsibility to monitor a clock or their watches and observe the times when Group A members raise their hands. Some will indicate the conclusion of three minutes before 90 seconds has elapsed. Five or six minutes will pass before others raise their hands for the final time. Group B should discuss their observations with the entire group. You may want to point out that this exercise focuses on a very short period of time with concentration on the task at hand. If one is in an unfamiliar environment without an accurate watch and involved in an exciting activity, it is easy to lose track of time. This can lead to being caught in the dark and contribute to becoming "lost."

Exercise 2 (Direction and Distance): (This exercise requires a large playfield or meadow. A football field would be a minimum size.) Now it is Group B's turn to put on the blindfolds. You "square off" the first blindfolded individual so that he/she is facing a selected point at least 100 yards away. The blindfolded individual is directed to walk a straight line to that point. Start the next individual from the same point after the previous walker is over 50 feet away. When they think they have arrived, they can quietly remove the blindfold but should remain at that point. The blindfolded walker from Group B is accompanied by a partner from Group A. The Group A partner is present for the purposes of safety and observation. The Group A partner is instructed not to touch or talk to the blindfolded person unless they are in danger of stepping into a hole, running into a fence, etc. The sighted partner from Group A also keeps track of the path the blindfolded person takes.

Most blindfolded walkers will begin to veer to the right or left of their goal. Some will make a number of corrections and overcorrections during their journey. Some will end up behind the point from which they started. Hence the thought of being lost and walking in circles. It happens.

Pull the whole group together and discuss their observations. Point out the human inadequacy of being able to walk a straight line and estimate distance even when we have our sight and landmarks are available for reference points. Relate what they have just experienced to traveling in the dark, dense forest, fog, or a whiteout.

VARIATIONS:
    1. Combine Exercises 1 and 2. The blindfolded walker indicates time intervals while moving toward the goal.
    2. The untracked beach, sand dune area, or snow covered field offers an ideal location for Exercise 2. You now have the added advantage of the blindfolded persons being able to have a visual record of the path they just wandered. Most will be surprised!
    3. Adapt the activity by using canoes or rowboats on a lake. Snow shoes, cross-country skis, or ice skates can also add an interesting twist.

SPECIAL SKILLS NEEDED FOR PARTICIPATION: None except for those obvious in Variation 3.

GROUP SIZE: Minimum of eight. Maximum of 30.

AGE GROUP: Seven and older.

NUMBER OF FACILITATORS: One.

DESCRIPTION OF EQUIPMENT AND FACILITIES:
    1. Large open area.
    2. Blindfolds.
    3. Clocks or watches.

SAFETY AND ENVIRONMENTAL CONSIDERATIONS: Exercise 2 requires an open area which is relatively free of natural and artificial hazards. The blindfolded persons need to know that this is not a race. They are to walk! You must impress on the sighted partners their responsibility for keeping the blindfolded walker out of danger.

TIME REQUIREMENT: One hour.

ACTIVITY TITLE: Use a Watch to Find North

GENERAL DESCRIPTION AND OBJECTIVES: This activity gives the student the skill and knowledge to estimate direction by using a wrist watch. A secondary educational objective for the facilitator to consider is that this activity provides an opening for discussion of the relationship of time to the rotation of the Earth. The language used by the facilitator must be very specific. And, when repeated, it must be repeated exactly. Efforts to explain the process in an alternate form generally lead to confusion.

Use the following description: "Hold the watch at arm's length, at chest level, in the palm of your hand with the face of the watch visible. Look from your eyes to the center of the watch to the end of the hour hand to the sun. This is our first line. Without moving the watch, visualize a line from the center of the watch to the 12. This is your second line. These two lines intersect at the center of the watch and form an angle. Bisect that angle with a third line. The end of the third line which is away from the center of the watch is approximately south. Face in that direction. Now north is to your back—east to your left—and west to your right."

(Note: Be prepared to deal with the issue of daylight saving time and the function of time zones.)

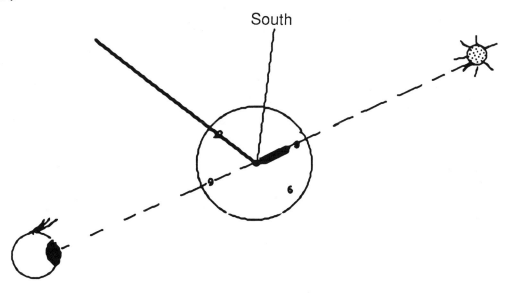

South

VARIATIONS: The Stick 'n Shadow Compass
Giant Sundial

SPECIAL SKILLS NEEDED FOR PARTICIPATION: None.

GROUP SIZE: This activity can be explained to a very large group. The facilitator(s), however, should work on an individual basis with the learner, explaining and demonstrating the process.

31

AGE GROUP: Ten years and older.

NUMBER OF FACILITATORS: One.

DESCRIPTION OF EQUIPMENT AND FACILITIES: It is handy to have the sun visible and be somewhere in the northern hemisphere. For a large group explanation and demonstration prior to individual work, a large cardboard or plywood "clock" aids the instruction. Some of the learners in your group will have digital watches. The system will work. Learners will, however, have to imagine the location of the clock's face numbers and the location of the hour hand.

SAFETY CONSIDERATION: Avoid having the learners look directly at the sun.

TIME REQUIREMENT: A minimum of 15 minutes.

ACTIVITY TITLE: The Stick 'n Shadow Compass

GENERAL DESCRIPTION AND OBJECTIVE(S): This is a variation of the activity entitled "Use a Watch to Find North." The objectives are similar. The tools used to find direction are different. We now have no compass and we have no wach. We do have sunshine, a flat and open area of land, and our brainpower. (Refer to drawing on next page.)

    1. Place a stick in the ground. The ground should be flat and horizontal. The stick should be vertical to the ground.
    2. The end of the stick's shadow which is away from the base of the stick is marked with a stone.
    3. Wait approximately 20 minutes. (Which way is the end of the shadow going to move? What direction is that? Which way does the sun move? East to west or west to east? Really! Which way does the earth rotate? At what rate? Is the shadow going to get longer or shorter? What time of day is it when the shadow is the shortest?)
    4. Now mark the end of the shadow with another stone. (Which way did the shadow move? Which stone is west and which is east?)
    5. Make a straight line between the two stones.
    6. Draw another straight line perpendicular to the first line.
    7. Which way is north?

VARIATIONS: Use a Watch to Find North

SPECIAL SKILLS NEEDED FOR PARTICIPATION: None.

GROUP SIZE: Ten or less.

AGE GROUP: Ten years and older.

NUMBER OF FACILITATORS: One facilitator for each group of ten.

DESCRIPTION OF EQUIPMENT AND FACILITIES:
1. A flat, open land space.
2. A five- to six-foot straight stick strong enough to be stuck into the ground or supported at the base with rocks.
3. Ten feet of string or rope to mark the lines.
4. A compass to check the results.

SAFETY AND ENVIRONMENTAL CONSIDERATIONS:
1. Avoid looking at the sun.
2. Limit the size of the stick to what is suggested. A couple of 14-year-olds sent to find a stick may return with a 12-foot log. Getting the log vertical and stable for 20 minutes may present a hazard.

TIME REQUIREMENT: Forty-five minutes. This allows time for introduction and a repeat of the process.

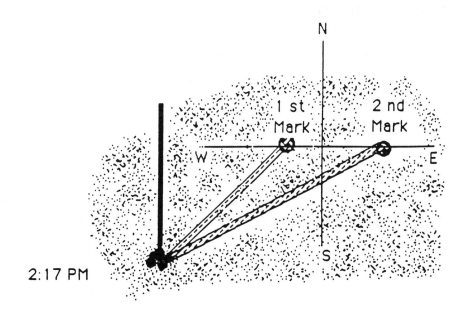

ACTIVITY TITLE: Human Compass

GENERAL DESCRIPTION AND OBJECTIVE(S): This is an activity appropriate for beginning compass users. It can also be used as an exercise to check whether or not self-proclaimed compass users really know what they are doing or not. (If you ask an average group of adults if they know how to use a compass, most will give you an affirmative response. When asked to perform in this activity, however, they say, "Well, it's been a long time." "I did it in the Scouts.")

The objective is to allow the participants to begin to recognize the process of reading "bearings" or an "azimuth." The person in the center is asked to read the bearing or azimuth which directs them to Hazel, then Arnold, then Harry, etc. If the person leaves the compass fixed and moves around the compass to make the readings, you know that they know correct usage. If the person in the center remains in a fixed position and moves the compass, you know they do not understand.

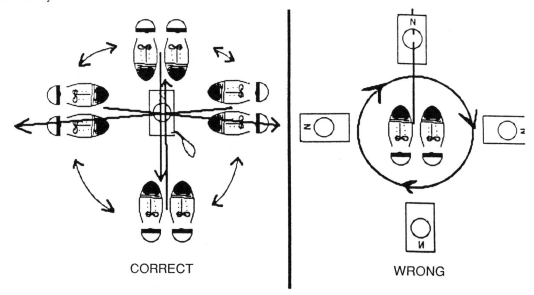

CORRECT   WRONG

VARIATIONS: Have the group on the parameter of the circle "read a bearing" to the person in the center of the circle. The person in the center of the circle then gives a "reverse bearing" or a back sighting to each person in the group (plus or minus 180 degrees, assuming you are using standard 360 degree compasses).

SPECIAL SKILLS NEEDED FOR PARTICIPATION: Basic orientation to the compass, how it works, cardinal points, intercardinal points.

GROUP SIZE: Twelve per group.

AGE GROUP: Eleven and older.

NUMBER OF FACILITATORS: One.

DESCRIPTION OF EQUIPMENT AND FACILITIES:
    1. A compass for each person or pair of participants.
    2. A large cardboard "compass" to use for demonstration.

TIME REQUIREMENT: Thirty minutes.

ACTIVITY TITLE: To Walk a Straight Line

GENERAL DESCRIPTION AND OBJECTIVE(S): The primary objective is for the learner to establish a bearing (or direction of travel) based on a compass reading and to follow that straight line for a prescribed distance to attain a preselected goal. When the goal can be seen from the initial point where the compass reading was established, there is no problem. When obstacles interfere with line of sight or direct travel, however, new skills are needed. This becomes a necessary skill to acquire prior to attempting an orienteering course.

In the case of thick forest cover, a technique is to travel in pairs. One person views the compass while the other travels the "bearing" to the most distant point which can be seen by person number one. Person number one directs person number two (left and right) to position themselves properly on the correct line of travel. Person number one then paces the distance from the starting point to person number two. The process is repeated until the goal is attained.

Another problem is when an obstacle which obstructs both line of sight and line of travel must be bypassed. In this case, a parallel bearing must be established. See illustration below.

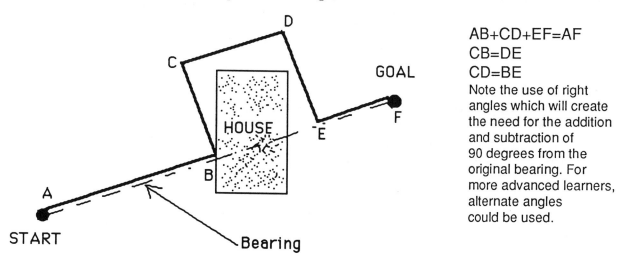

AB+CD+EF=AF
CB=DE
CD=BE
Note the use of right angles which will create the need for the addition and subtraction of 90 degrees from the original bearing. For more advanced learners, alternate angles could be used.

SPECIAL SKILLS NEEDED FOR PARTICIPATION: Compass and pacing literacy.

GROUP SIZE: Work in pairs.

AGE GROUP: Over 12 years old.

NUMBER OF FACILITATORS: Based on number of participants and environment.

DESCRIPTION OF EQUIPMENT AND FACILITIES: One compass per pair.

TIME REQUIREMENT: One hour minimum.

ACTIVITY TITLE: Compass/Disc-Golf

GENERAL DESCRIPTION AND OBJECTIVE(S): This activity combines compass skills with the game of Disc-Golf (Frisbie Golf). The objectives include use of the compass, fun, and fitness.

Disc-Golf requires the players to toss the disc from "tee one" to "hole one" and record the number of tosses. A par, of course, has been established and the player or team with the lowest score wins. Compass/Disc-Golf is played in a similar manner except that the locations of the "holes" are listed in reference to bearing or azimuth and distance. In other words, the players do not have known "holes" and must use their compass and estimation of distance skills in order to find the "hole" and directions to the next "hole." Score is based on number of tosses.

This sounds fairly easy. If the player is accurate enough with each toss so that the disc lands on the "bearing line," the game is easy. If, however, the wind drifts the disc sixty feet to one side, now the compass work, math, and problem solving become more difficult. Make certain the players have the skills and understanding to participate in this activity. If they do not, the enjoyable objective of fun turns to ugly frustration.

VARIATIONS:
1. Score the game combining the number of tosses with points also given for time. Think this one out. Your objective is to get the individuals running, but not so that the compass work or distance estimation is jeopardized.
2. Have the players toss a disc as far as they can. They record a bearing and distance from the point the disc was tossed to the point it landed. Repeat this process X times. The data collected can be placed on an "oriented" graph and result, in effect, in the creation of a basic map.

3. Turn the "holes" into clues which lead to a treasure.
4. Forget the disc and use the compass as the tool to find the treasure.

SPECIAL SKILLS NEEDED FOR PARTICIPATION:
      1. Mastery of reading the compass (see Human Compass).
      2. Mastery of pacing (see Estimating Measurements).
      3. Experience in walking a bearing (see To Walk a Straight Line).

GROUP SIZE: One player per team or pairs or a team of three. After three all would not be participating.

AGE GROUP: Fifteen and older.

NUMBER OF FACILITATORS: One.

DESCRIPTION OF EQUIPMENT AND FACILITIES:
      1. Compass for each team.
      2. Disc for each team.
      3. Pencil and paper.
      4. A method of marking holes.
      5. A large outdoor area which allows the holes to be hidden from the tees.

SAFETY AND ENVIRONMENTAL CONSIDERATIONS: The toss of the disc puts an unknown variable into the facilitator's control of the activity. What if it goes in the river? Or on top of someone's roof? What if a team gets "turned around" 180 degrees? Think about the worst possible scenario and provide rules to keep the game safe and with minimum impact on the environment.

TIME REQUIREMENT: Variable. The number of holes, the length of each hole, the ability of the slowest player, and type of terrain will determine the required time. The facilitator should pretest the course.

ACTIVITY TITLE: Topo Maps

GENERAL DESCRIPTION AND OBJECTIVE(S): Topographical maps of backcountry areas are a prime tool both for planning a trip and for use during the trip itself. For some they can also be a source of frustration in that the user cannot "see" how the map works. The objective of this activity is to give the participant a basic understanding of how topographical maps work so that they can "see" the strengths and weaknesses of the tool.

Step 1. Obtain topo maps of an area familiar to the participants. Take the group to a vantage point where significant landmarks can be sighted (road intersections, lakes, a railroad, major structures). Have them orient the map to match the land which the map represents. Check their orientation with a compass. Discuss distances and relate those observations to the scale of the map. Look at elevation differences and relate them to the contour lines on the map. What does the map do a good job of depicting? What significant real elements are not represented on the map?

Step 2. Option A—Place an old bed sheet over a chair. With an ink marker, draw "contour lines" completely around your sheet mountain, parallel to the floor, for each two inches of elevation. Have the participants stand on tables so that they can look down on to the sheet and draw a topo map of what they see. A quick glance at the maps will let you know if the individual understands the relationship between the actual mountain and the map. Quiz them. Have them point out specific ridges, gullies, etc. Challenge them. Have them develop a scale and contour intervals. Have them indicate both true north and magnetic north.

Option B—Make a "mountain" out of sand. Use string for the contour lines.

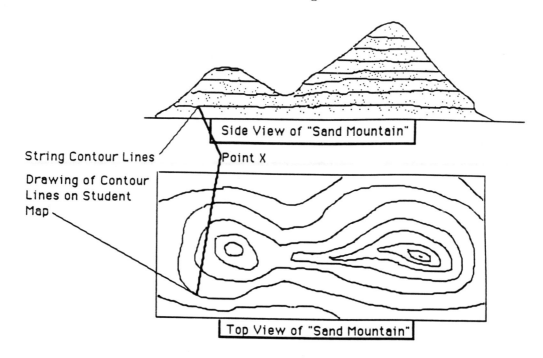

Side View of "Sand Mountain"

String Contour Lines

Point X

Drawing of Contour Lines on Student Map

Top View of "Sand Mountain"

38

VARIATIONS: If the group has a basic understanding of topographical maps along with some experience using them, introduce this variation. Provide a group of four with a topo map of a wilderness area which is unfamiliar to them. Mark a point A and a point B on the map. The distance between should be at least twenty-five miles. Have the group select the best back-packing (horse, cross-country skiing, mountain biking) route from point A to point B. What is the distance of this route? What is the elevation gain? What is the elevation loss? How long will it take the group to make the trip? If they need to camp, where will their site be? Why? Where will they plan to get water? What information would they like to have about the selected route that the map does not give them?

The strength of this activity is greatly increased, of course, if the group is able to test their planning by actually doing the route.

SPECIAL SKILLS NEEDED FOR PARTICIPATION: Basic compass skills. An understanding of the variation between magnetic and true north.

GROUP SIZE: An individual activity if possible. More than four participants using a map becomes cumbersome.

AGE GROUP: Twelve years and older.

NUMBER OF FACILITATORS: One for each ten participants.

DESCRIPTION OF EQUIPMENT AND FACILITIES: U.S. Geological Survey or park service quads. Straight edge. Pencils. Compass.

TIME REQUIREMENT: Ninety-minute time block.

Chapter 5

Outdoor Recreation Activities With Academic Application

ACTIVITY TITLE: Estimating Measurements

GENERAL DESCRIPTION AND OBJECTIVE(S): Many people are uncomfortable making estimates of distance and size in the outdoors without the tools normally at hand. They ask, "How far is it?" The question is there and, therefore the opportunity to give a known answer or to use the inquiry as an opportunity for more significant learning.

This activity provides participants with the opportunity to individually learn to estimate linear distance.

Start with the individual's body. How tall are they? What is their "wing span" (fingertip to fingertip)? What is the relationship between those two measurements? How high can they reach up a wall with outstretched arms? What is the distance from fingertip to elbow? How long are the knuckles on their fingers? What is the distance from the end of the little finger to the end of the thumb with the hand spread? How long is their foot?

With the answers to these questions in mind, we can test the accuracy of our measurements. For example, the circumference of a large tree can be estimated by having a group "hug" the tree with fingertips of each individual just touching. The height of a cliff can be estimated by breaking it down into sections the height or double the height of the individual. Try this approach and be ready to compare the estimations to actual distance.

(Caution: Do not let the measurement of body parts get out of control especially when working with teenagers.)

VARIATIONS: 1. Pacing. The objective is for participants to learn about their "normal walking pace" (each step or each time the right foot makes contact). Have the individuals walk a premeasured 100 feet or 100 yards counting their paces. This should be done five to ten times with an average established and the math applied to figure the distance of one pace. Individual conversion charts might be developed for 10 feet, 50 yards, etc.

If you are going to get into hikes, backpacking, and/or orienteering, pacing becomes a bit more sophisticated. The normal walking pace has some modifications depending on such variables as slope of the terrain, the walking surface, the time of day, and the load being carried. Have your group walk a half-mile section of trail which includes uphill, downhill, sandy soil, rock, mud, and maybe a few obstacles such as logs across the trail. Repeat this process at least three times. Count the paces and/or keep track of time. This activity will assist in giving the individuals and the group an appreciation of distance and the amount of time it will take the group to cover a selected route. The group should leave this activity knowing about how fast they travel and how far a mile is. If they plan a backpacking trip with an estimation that they will carry loaded packs in mountainous terrain at an average speed of seven miles per hour, repeat the activity!

2. What is a square foot, a square mile, an acre? Show the group.

SPECIAL SKILLS NEEDED FOR PARTICIPATION: None.

GROUP SIZE: This is an activity which can be done individually or in small groups. The opportunity to compare results of estimations needs to be considered.

AGE GROUP: Ten years and older.

NUMBER OF FACILITATORS: One.

DESCRIPTION OF EQUIPMENT AND FACILITIES:
1. Measuring tape(s).
2. Known distances of examples to be used for estimation.

TIME REQUIREMENT: Variable. This can be a spur of the moment exercise or an extended activity.

ACTIVITY TITLE: How Tall Is That Tree?

GENERAL DESCRIPTION AND OBJECTIVE(S): The primary objective is to estimate the height of a tree by applying some geometry skills. Have the participants estimate the height of a specific tree or a number of trees and record those estimations. Next, have the individuals form pairs. Person one stands between the tree in question and person two. The pair moves until the top of the tree is "in line" with the top of person one's head as viewed by person two's eye from the ground.

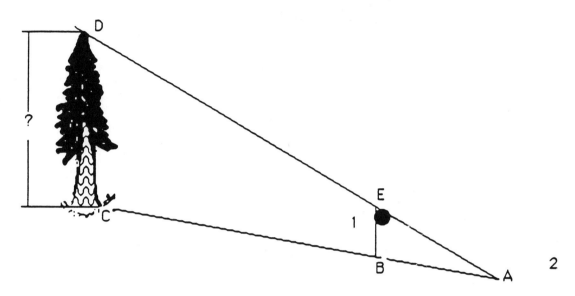

The distance between A and B is to the height of person one as the distance between A and C is to the height of the tree (AB=BE and AC=CD). Now the pair has access to a distance they can measure with a tape or pace off—AC equals the tree height. Check the results with the original estimation.

VARIATIONS:
1. Have the participants experiment with this technique with some object with a known height (basketball rim, goal post cross-bar, etc.). Let them see how accurate they are.

2. Have the participants "cut down" the tree with their imagination and a stick. Hold a foot-long stick at arm's length (position Al). Sight the top of the tree (B) so that it lines up with the top of the stick and the base of the tree so that it lines up with the hand holding the stick. Now, with the hand and base of tree still in line, rotate the top of the stick (from its line with top of the tree, B) to the ground (B1). Mark that spot. Measure from that spot to the base of the tree.

SPECIAL SKILLS NEEDED FOR PARTICIPATION: None.

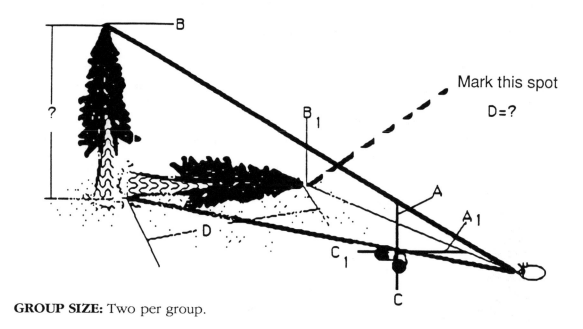

Mark this spot

D=?

GROUP SIZE: Two per group.

AGE GROUP: Ten years and older.

NUMBER OF FACILITATORS: One.

DESCRIPTION OF EQUIPMENT AND FACILITIES:
1. Any inaccessible tall object located on flat accessible ground.
2. Measuring tape.

SAFETY AND ENVIRONMENTAL CONSIDERATIONS: Don't cut the tree down to check the height.

TIME REQUIREMENT: Fifteen minutes.

ACTIVITY TITLE: Boat Race

GENERAL DESCRIPTION AND OBJECTIVE(S): Many of us are interested in or at least curious about speed. How fast are we going? How fast is the water flowing? This activity offers the participant the opportunity to answer one or both of these questions.

In its simplest form, a floating object is placed in a river or stream at point A. The object is allowed to travel for ten seconds. The point which the object has reached at the end of ten seconds becomes point B. The distance between point A and point B is measured. The distance traveled is now known and the time it took to travel that distance is known. Distance divided by time equals speed (D/T = S). For example, if the object traveled forty feet during the ten-second period, the conversion would be 240 feet for one minute or 14,400 feet for an hour. Divide 14,400 by 5,280 (feet per statute mile) for a result of 2.7 miles per hour (average speed).

Most of us are tuned into miles per hour. The unit of time used, therefore, should be one which is easy to convert from seconds or minutes to an hour.

VARIATIONS:
1. Use a premeasured distance from point A to point B as the constant as opposed to time as the constant and then record the time.
2. Build various types of "boats." Which are faster? Big ones? Small ones? Heavy? Light?
3. The activity can be modified to see how fast one is skiing, ice skating, sledding, etc.
4. By placing a float in the water next to a moving 16-foot canoe and recording the time it takes to reach the stern, the speed of the canoe can be established. For example, if the time elapsed was 3.7 seconds we know the boat speed was approximately 3 miles per hour (5,280 feet/16 = 330; 330 x 3.7 seconds = 1,221 seconds; 1,221/60 = 20.35 minutes; 20.35/60 = .34 of an hour; 3 x .34 = 1.01 hours; 3 x 1 mile = 3 miles).

SPECIAL SKILLS NEEDED FOR PARTICIPATION: Math skills appropriate for the approach the facilitator elects.

GROUP SIZE: Open.

AGE GROUP: This depends upon facilitator approach. Junior high school and high school aged students should be able to be presented with the problem and figure out a method for solution. Most ten-year-olds would need a conversion chart.

NUMBER OF FACILITATORS: One.

DESCRIPTION OF EQUIPMENT AND FACILITIES:
1. Moving water.
2. Floating objects.
3. Stop watch.
4. Conversion charts.

SAFETY AND ENVIRONMENTAL CONSIDERATIONS: Moving water has the potential of being dangerous. Common sense in the selection of the site is called for. If paper boats or aluminum cans are used as the floating objects, a method of recovering them is required.

TIME REQUIREMENT:
1. Thirty minutes for collection of data.
2. Calculation time will vary depending upon the age group, their skills, and the facilitator approach.

ACTIVITY TITLE: Heads or Tails Hike

GENERAL DESCRIPTION AND OBJECTIVE(S): As an awareness activity, the Heads or Tails Hike is pretty tough to beat. It not only causes participants to be aware of their surroundings as they explore new areas, but also puts them in a situation where they need to cooperate with each other.

The principle behind the Heads or Tails Hike is pretty basic. The participants begin hiking down a road or trail. Every time there is a fork or a side road, they must flip a coin. If the coin lands heads, the group goes right. If it's tails, they go to the left. It is important that the group makes a map while they are on their trek. This not only helps them observe their surroundings but it might also be useful in getting them back to their starting point.

Groups tend to work better for this activity if they are kept relatively small. This way, the participants feel as if they are taking a more active part in the hike than just merely following the masses. One can be in charge of flipping the coin, another in charge of the compass, another draws the map, etc.

VARIATIONS: Upstream/Downstream Hike

SPECIAL SKILLS NEEDED FOR PARTICIPATION: None really, but a basic knowledge of map and compass will not only increase participants' confidence but allow them to venture a little further than they normally would without those skills.

GROUP SIZE: Not more than six.

AGE GROUP: Twelve years or older.

NUMBER OF FACILITATORS: One for every two or three groups.

DESCRIPTION OF EQUIPMENT AND FACILITIES:
1. One coin per group.
2. Pencil and paper.
3. At least one compass per group.

SAFETY AND ENVIRONMENTAL CONSIDERATIONS: In planning this activity, the facilitator needs to be familiar with the area in which the group will be hiking in order to alleviate any hazards or minimize the possibility of a group getting disoriented.

TIME REQUIREMENT: At least one hour.

ACTIVITY TITLE: Upstream/Downstream Hike

GENERAL DESCRIPTION AND OBJECTIVE(S): When studying wildlife, there's not a better place to begin than along a streambed. Participants can choose whether to hike up or down stream, but must make notes of wildlife signs and sightings along the way. At the conclusion of the hike, facilitators can use what participants have observed as a foundation for discussions on local wildlife habitat, conservation, etc.

Younger participants often seem to equate the term wildlife with visions of deer, foxes, bear, or other large animals. This activity can be useful in pointing out other important members of the animal kingdom, such as the tiny aquatic insects found flitting above the water or the mayfly nymphs underneath the rocks in the stream.

VARIATIONS: Heads or Tails Hike
Photo Safari

SPECIAL SKILLS NEEDED FOR PARTICIPATION: None.

GROUP SIZE: Relatively small. No more than six.

AGE GROUP: Ten years or older.

NUMBER OF FACILITATORS: For younger groups, there should probably be one facilitator per group. If the groups are old enough to venture out on their own, one facilitator for every three groups is usually sufficient.

DESCRIPTION OF EQUIPMENT AND FACILITIES:
1. An area that has an accessible streambed.
2. Notebooks and pencils.

SAFETY AND ENVIRONMENTAL CONSIDERATIONS: Naturally, there is always a concern for safety when the activity takes place around water. In this activity, there is also the environmental concern of disrupting a streambed. Common sense, care, and consideration should be emphasized to participants before they begin.

TIME REQUIREMENT: Allow at least one hour, especially in an area where there is an abundance of wildlife.

ACTIVITY TITLE: Photo Safari

GENERAL DESCRIPTION AND OBJECTIVE(S): The objectives of this activity are very similar to those of the Upstream/Downstream Hike. Participants should become more aware of wildlife and the importance of protecting wildlife habitat.

The Photo Safari is a directed hike where participants try to take pictures of wildlife. This activity demands patience, because participants will find that in order to get good pictures, they have to be quiet and willing to wait.

If participants have access to a Polaroid or other similar type camera, the finished pictures can lead to discussions about the various types of wildlife observed and their characteristics. If a Polaroid is not available, this gives everyone a good excuse to get together at a later date and look at each other's photos or slides.

VARIATIONS: Upstream/Downstream Hike

SPECIAL SKILLS NEEDED FOR PARTICIPATION: While some photographic skills might be helpful, this activity can be used with participants whose only knowledge of a camera is to aim and shoot.

GROUP SIZE: This can vary. While a small group of five or six is ideal, this activity can be modified for that one individual who enjoys taking pictures or for the larger group who enjoy photographing wildlife.

AGE GROUP: Twelve and older.

NUMBER OF FACILITATORS: One.

DESCRIPTION OF EQUIPMENT AND FACILITIES:
1. One camera per participant is ideal. One camera per group will work but occasional hard feelings creep up as to who gets to take the pictures. Even with adult groups, participants enjoy snapping the shot.

SAFETY AND ENVIRONMENTAL CONSIDERATIONS: While taking a picture of a Stellar's jay nibbling on a bread crust seems fairly safe, getting that close-up of a bear cub is not only foolhardy but can prove to be downright dangerous. Even members of the seemingly gentle deer family can be very aggressive when provoked by a zealous shutterbug. If participants lack sophisticated telephoto equipment, it is probably best to take the long shot and explain it later with the aid of a magnifying glass.

TIME REQUIREMENT: This is the type of activity that can be limited to one hour or can be part of a participant's free time for several weeks. It's up to you.

ACTIVITY TITLE: Giant Sundial

GENERAL DESCRIPTION AND OBJECTIVE(S): How does the earth rotate in its relationship to the sun? This simple activity gives participants an idea of the earth's rotation in addition to the added benefit of having a big "clock" with which to tell time.

In order to have accurate time, it is important to find or prepare a large level area, away from overshadowing trees or obstacles. A sundial can be different sizes, of course, but making a large one seems to keep interest levels high.

An eight- to ten-foot pole is usually a good size for the sundial's style, providing it is straight. To begin, set the pole in the ground at an angle facing north. The depth of the hole should be approximately two to three feet, with the dirt packed fairly loosely around the pole in order to make final adjustments. When this is accomplished, wait until dark, then slant the pole to the north until the tip is aligned directly with the North Star. Pack the dirt firmly around the base and make a final check by sighting along the pole to make sure the style has not shifted in its position.

The angle of sight from where you stand to the North Star corresponds to the latitude of your location. As a result, a sundial can also be made by knowing latitude and setting the style at the angle, pointing true north.

After the style has been set at the proper angle and direction, the hour marks can be set in a circle around the style. Probably the easiest way to do this is with a plumb line. Attach the plumb line to the tip of the style and drive a peg directly below it. Providing the style is set properly the style's shadow should cover the peg at twelve o'clock, noon. By using a watch, hour marks can be precisely made by driving a peg in the center of the shadow for every hour that has enough sunlight to make a reading.

It might be well to note that if this activity is conducted during daylight saving time, the plumb line will be hovering over the one o'clock peg. This fact, though, can lead into other questions the facilitator might use in order to stimulate participant curiosity.

NORTH

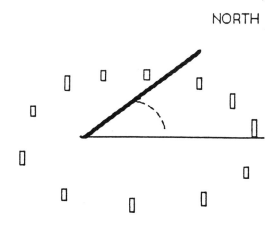

VARIATIONS: The Stick 'n Shadow Compass
Use a Watch to Find North

SPECIAL SKILLS NEEDED FOR PARTICIPATION: None.

GROUP SIZE: Five or six is about right. While this activity might be interesting to a larger group, most participants would wind up merely being spectators.

AGE GROUP: Ten years and older.

NUMBER OF FACILITATORS: One.

DESCRIPTION OF EQUIPMENT AND FACILITIES:
1. A large, open, level area.
2. An eight- to ten-foot pole.
3. Twelve to 15 pegs.

TIME REQUIREMENT: A nice thing about this activity is that once the style is positioned, participants can be involved in other activities, only returning once every hour to mark shadows.

ACTIVITY TITLE: Scavengers' Nature Hike

GENERAL DESCRIPTION AND OBJECTIVE(S): This activity is good in helping participants become aware of their surroundings. It can also be used as an effective springboard into a discussion on biology or natural history.

Participants are divided into groups, preparatory to going on a short nature hike. Prior to leaving on the hike, each group should receive a list of nature objects that they are apt to find in the area: leaves, seeds, feathers, nuts, and other collectible items. If it is preferred that participants don't collect the items on the list, a facilitator can go with each group to check off items as the group discovers them. The object is to collect or observe as many of the objects as possible.

VARIATIONS: Follow the Track
Super Sleuth Hike

SPECIAL SKILLS NEEDED FOR PARTICIPATION: None, just a willingness to learn and observe.

GROUP SIZE: Six to eight participants per group. Any more than five groups of participants might be a little too much for one facilitator to supervise.

AGE GROUP: Eight years to 12 years of age seems to work pretty well. While older students can find this activity interesting, the enthusiasm level doesn't seem to be as high as with the younger groups.

NUMBER OF FACILITATORS: One for every five groups of participants.

DESCRIPTION OF EQUIPMENT AND FACILITIES:
1. Any outdoor area large enough to facilitate a 20-minute nature hike (not including observation or discussion time).
2. Sheet of paper for each group listing items to either collect or observe.

SAFETY AND ENVIRONMENTAL CONSIDERATIONS: The hike route should be carefully planned in order to avoid impact on environmentally sensitive areas. Lists should include only those items that could either be collected or observed without affecting the environment negatively.

TIME REQUIREMENT: While the entire distance of the hike should be able to be covered within twenty minutes, the facilitator should probably allow 45 minutes to an hour in order to accommodate observations or searching time.

ACTIVITY TITLE: Super Sleuth Hike

GENERAL DESCRIPTION AND OBJECTIVE(S): With some careful planning on the part of the facilitator, this activity will not only cause the participants to be observant along a designated nature trail but also aid in their learning the objectives the facilitator has previously outlined.

To begin, each group of participants is given four or five numbered and sealed envelopes containing instructions for the hike. The first envelope directs participants to a stopping area where they may open the second envelope, which gives them instructions on a task to perform. For example, "By counting the rings on the big stump in front of you, how old would you say the tree was when it was cut down?" The second envelope also directs them to the next stopping place where they are to open a third envelope, and so forth. The sealed instructions should be geared to the level of the age or knowledge of the participants. Other examples of instructions might include: "Notice the hole dug into the side of the riverbank. What kind of animal do you think made that hole? Why?"

The final envelope should direct the participants back to the starting point where all observations can be noted and discussed. The facilitator can then answer any questions about what was observed or direct attention to a certain area of the hike for additional discussion.

VARIATIONS: Scavengers' Nature Hike
Follow the Track

SPECIAL SKILLS NEEDED FOR PARTICIPATION: None.

GROUP SIZE: Five or six.

AGE GROUP: Eight to twelve years old.

NUMBER OF FACILITATORS: One facilitator can usually handle two or three groups if they are sent out on their own. If the age or maturity level of the group is such that the facilitator would feel more comfortable going with them, then one facilitator per group is needed.

DESCRIPTION OF EQUIPMENT AND FACILITIES: Large area that would facilitate a reasonable nature hike. For younger children, one mile in length is usually sufficient.

SAFETY AND ENVIRONMENTAL CONSIDERATIONS: The trail should be planned through an area where the hiking of several participants would not cause environmental damage.

TIME REQUIREMENT: Forty-five minutes to an hour.

ACTIVITY TITLE: Follow the Track

GENERAL DESCRIPTION AND OBJECTIVE(S): This activity can teach participants observation skills either by looking for actual animal tracks or by following tracks made by the facilitator or another member of the group. If following actual animal tracks, the facilitator might want to instruct participants on how to make plaster casts, or perhaps have the participants make sketches of the tracks. If there are no signs of animals around, the facilitator or another participant can lay down a track by marking an "X" with chalk on rocks along the trail or by attaching a rope to a small log with nails driven in part way and dragging it behind them. Participants are then to follow the track to where the "trackee" leads them.

VARIATIONS: Super Sleuth Hike
Scavengers' Nature Hike

SPECIAL SKILLS NEEDED FOR PARTICIPATION: None.

GROUP SIZE: Six to eight participants per group

AGE GROUP: Eight to 12 years of age.

NUMBER OF FACILITATORS: One is usually plenty.

DESCRIPTION OF EQUIPMENT AND FACILITIES:
     1. Plaster, paper cups for mixing, small sticks for stirring if using actual animal tracks and making casts.
     2. Paper and pencils if participants are going to make sketches of tracks.
     3. If human-made tracks are used, a tracking log with rope or chalk will be needed.

SAFETY AND ENVIRONMENTAL CONSIDERATIONS: If laying down a track with a tracking log, care must be taken to avoid environmentally sensitive areas.

TIME REQUIREMENT: Thirty to 45 minutes.

Chapter 6

Outdoor Physical Fitness Activities

ACTIVITY TITLE: Dry Land Skiing

GENERAL DESCRIPTION AND OBJECTIVE(S): As an alternative to the old "take a couple of laps," participants can grab a set of ski poles and take a run up and down the hills of a park or forest area. This can be a lot of fun. The downhill portions can include a slalom course around trees, rocks, or artificial obstacles such as traffic cones.

The physical fitness objectives include an increase in aerobic fitness, strength, agility, and endurance. The poling action on the hills adds some uncommon upper body action to this running activity.

SPECIAL SKILLS NEEDED FOR PARTICIPATION: None.

GROUP SIZE: Open.

AGE GROUP: Seven and older.

NUMBER OF FACILITATORS: One.

DESCRIPTION OF EQUIPMENT AND FACILITIES:

1. Ski poles or sections of doweling.
2. Hillside.

SAFETY AND ENVIRONMENTAL CONSIDERATIONS:

1. A little follow the leader with the facilitator being the leader will keep the downhill runs under control. Of course, this means the facilitator should be in good enough physical shape to do what is being asked of the participants.

2. Site selection should be considered. Charging about in a botanical garden will draw some negative comment. Cutting across established trails may encourage erosion.

3. Use an area which is free of other users. Twenty running teenagers armed with ski poles can be a frightening sight and potentially dangerous to the local seniors garden club out on their daily walk.

TIME REQUIREMENT: Open.

ACTIVITY TITLE: Pony Express

GENERAL DESCRIPTION AND OBJECTIVE(S): This activity demonstrates how communications can be misinterpreted as they are passed from one individual to another. It helps emphasize the need for effective communication skills.

Pony Express is an outdoor variation of the old party game "Telephone," where participants whisper a message from one person to another until the message gets all the way around the room. Usually, the final message is completely different from what was originally started. Pony Express is no different except for the fact that participants are outdoors and must travel (walk fast or run) a designated distance before they can pass the verbal message to another group member. Group members can be situated anywhere from fifty yards to a quarter mile apart, depending upon the age and abilities of the participants

Messages should be kept relatively simple, depending upon the group, yet involved enough to allow for the potential of miscommunication if the participants aren't careful. Nursery rhymes, limericks, or other nonsensical phrases can all be used as viable messages.

While this activity can be done with one large group, it has generally proved more successful when there are two or three groups competing against each other. With one group, there is the occasional "miscommunicator" who intentionally tries to foul up the communication. With two or more groups competing to see who gets the message to the final station first and most accurately, the potential for the "miscommunicator" is minimized.

VARIATIONS: The Invisible Leader
                    The Return of the Invisible Leader

SPECIAL SKILLS NEEDED FOR PARTICIPATION: None really, other than the ability to be ambulatory.

GROUP SIZE: Each group should have at least 12 to 15 participants in order for the activity to be successful and still fun. More than three groups would probably prove to be a real handful for most facilitators.

AGE GROUP: Eight years through 15 years old. While older participants have found this activity to be enjoyable, it usually finds maximum enjoyment with the younger participants.

NUMBER OF FACILITATORS: One is usually plenty unless the pony express course doesn't make a complete loop. In this case, another facilitator would be necessary in order to check to see if the messages were delivered correctly.

DESCRIPTION OF EQUIPMENT AND FACILITIES: The area should be relatively free from "hidden hazards" that would make rapid travel difficult or unsafe. The only equipment needed is a message to whisper into the ear of each #1 "rider."

SAFETY AND ENVIRONMENTAL CONSIDERATIONS: No matter how often facilitators emphasize being careful, there is always one "express rider" who is willing to "put spurs to the horse" no matter what the costs. As a result, the course should be laid where safety is maximized.

TIME REQUIREMENT: This can vary, but 30 to 45 minutes is usually quite sufficient, depending upon the size of the group and the length of the course.

ACTIVITY TITLE: The Educational-Inspirational-Fitness Trail

GENERAL DESCRIPTION AND OBJECTIVE(S): The common fitness trail is a form of circuit training where the individual or group performs a specific exercise at each station along the course. The objective is to provide a balance of exercises which match the components of physical fitness.

An often found form of an educational trail is one of an interpretive nature. For example, national and state parks provide trails with information about the history, flora, fauna, and/or geology of the area. Each station has printed information in the form of a sign or may have a number which directs participants to a corresponding number in a printed handout they carry with them.

VARIATIONS: This activity can have as much variation as the facilitator has imagination. The activity is fine as a straight fitness trail. It is fine as a straight educational trail with historical events, current events, spelling words, or math problems associated with each station. Or, one can combine the two approaches with the reading of a science concept just prior to and/or just after 20 sit-ups. Then on to the next station, science concept, and physical exercise.

Church schools and camps can use the concept with the inclusion of an inspirational passage at each of the stations.

SPECIAL SKILLS NEEDED FOR PARTICIPATION: The facilitator should match the exercise, educational material, and/or inspirational passages to the skill and maturity levels of the participants.

GROUP SIZE: Depending on the trail. The group can be very large or one individual can participate.

AGE GROUP: The activity can be adjusted to meet the needs of all age groups.

NUMBER OF FACILITATORS: One or none.

DESCRIPTION OF EQUIPMENT AND FACILITIES: The stations can be as simple as 5 x 7 cards posted on the fence of a school yard or as sophisticated and expensive as redwood plaques with information mounted under plexiglas.

SAFETY AND ENVIRONMENTAL CONSIDERATIONS: If the trail is less than straightforward or there is the chance of confusion, have the group work in pairs (minimum). If a permanent trail is designed, the environmental impact and aesthetics should be well thought out.

TIME REQUIREMENT: Twenty minutes to an hour.

ACTIVITY TITLE: The Break

GENERAL DESCRIPTION AND OBJECTIVE(S): The concept and practice of The Break come from the Hahnian schools (Salem and Gordenstoun), which have significant historical importance in experiential and service education. In these schools, Kurt Hahn instituted a break during the academic day for physical activities. The format for the activities was uniquely competitive while being cooperative. The competition was both self-competition and group competition. Success was measured by the percentage of improvement over a given period of time. Highly skilled athletes performing at their peak would only demonstrate limited gains in performance. The less skilled or younger athlete could provide the greatest percentage points for the team in that they had the most room to improve. A heterogeneous grouping of skilled and less skilled, mature and less mature, formed the individual teams. This system encouraged all team members to contribute to the team effort the best that they could. The system also had an inherent structure which allowed the skilled to help the less skilled. (A far cry from the choosing of teams that leaves the little fat kid always being chosen last!) Running, jumping, sit-ups, and pull-ups were included in the events.

The objectives include improvement in individual physical fitness, development of team spirit and cooperation, and a brief release from the academic classroom or sedate recreation activities.

SELECTED VARIATION: The American Alliance for Health, Physical Education, Recreation and Dance program, Physical Best (available from AAHPERD, 1900 Association Drive, Reston, VA 22091), provides a perfect basis for Break activities. The primary components of fitness are addressed in the testing program. Break activities could include measurements of improvement from the first test to the final test and/or weekly assessment.

SPECIAL SKILLS NEEDED FOR PARTICIPATION: None.

GROUP SIZE: Three to 12 participants per group.

AGE GROUP: The system works for all age groups or a mixed group of many ages.

NUMBER OF FACILITATORS: Only one is necessary. The bulk of the work is in preparation.

DESCRIPTION OF EQUIPMENT AND FACILITIES: Equipment and facilities can be as simple as a printed handout or a sophisticated system of sequential stations (see Educational/Inspirational/Fitness Trail).

TIME REQUIREMENT: Five to 30 minutes per occasion. The occasions may be a couple of times per day or once a week.

ACTIVITY TITLE: The Giant Relay

GENERAL DESCRIPTION AND OBJECTIVE(S): The Giant Relay allows all participants to be part of a team. In addition, the ideal situation lets each participant function in a skill area in which they are proficient. As an example, the first leg of the relay may be a 100-meter dash. The second leg might be a mile-long bicycle ride; the third, a group of six paddle across the pond in a canoe; the fourth, another run; the fifth, ten free throws at the basketball court; etc.

This activity can work well within the confines of a school yard—utilizing the resources at hand. Or it can be successful at a camp where equestrian and sailing activities may be included.

It is suggested that the event works best as a culminating activity—after the participants have been able to recognize the activities for which they have an affinity and some skill.

VARIATIONS: Tailored biathlons or triathlons
Pole, Pedal, and Paddle (a combination of cross-country skiing, bicycling, and canoeing/kayaking)

SPECIAL SKILLS NEEDED FOR PARTICIPATION: Those appropriate for the specific legs of the event.

GROUP SIZE: Variable.

AGE GROUP: Any or mixed.

NUMBER OF FACILITATORS: Dependent on group size, sophistication of event, and age and maturity level of participants.

DESCRIPTION OF EQUIPMENT AND FACILITIES: Variable.

SAFETY AND ENVIRONMENTAL CONSIDERATIONS: Be sure to have facilitators as supervisors and traffic directors at all critical points of the relay.

TIME REQUIREMENT: Variable.

ACTIVITY TITLE: Geographical Push-Ups

DESCRIPTION OF EQUIPMENT AND FACILITIES: A very large map of your state, the nation, or the world painted on a parking lot or playground surface. The minimum size should be 30 x 60 feet. This, of course, depends on the shape of the land mass your map will represent.

GENERAL DESCRIPTION AND OBJECTIVE(S): Have the participants place themselves at random points on the "map." (One per state, for example, on a U.S. map.) Then use the map as a circuit training tool: five push-ups in California, ten sit-ups in Texas, run in place for two minutes in New York, etc.

SPECIAL SKILLS NEEDED FOR PARTICIPATION: The participants need appropriate knowledge of the geography to be used and the exercises to be performed.

GROUP SIZE: Variable.

AGE GROUP: Minimum nine years of age. (Check the state curriculum mandates to know at which grade level the particular geography your map represents is studied.)

NUMBER OF FACILITATORS: One.

SAFETY AND ENVIRONMENTAL CONSIDERATIONS: Avoid making the activity a race where heads get bumped and egos bruised.

TIME REQUIREMENT: Variable.

ACTIVITY TITLE: Let's Improve

GENERAL DESCRIPTION AND OBJECTIVE(S): Children often become frustrated when trying to compete with those of greater athletic prowess. A modification of a ringer tournament, Let's Improve is a challenging way to develop individual skills without group pressures or frustrations of group competition.

This activity can be utilized with a variety of skill development areas. Initially, the facilitator should pair up the individuals in the group, either according to ability or social compatibility. Then, each pair is instructed to keep track of each other's progress in the selected skill area over a number of days or weeks, depending upon the time allowance determined by the facilitator. Only the best scores are totaled in the end.

The following chart helps to illustrate this concept, with making free throws in basketball. Chris and Kim have been paired to monitor each other's free throws. Every day, the two participants shoot ten free throws. The number registered on their scoring chart is the number of baskets made out of ten. During the second week, Kim made five of the attempted free throws on Monday and six of the attempted shots on Tuesday. Inasmuch as these scores are an improvement over Kim's previous scores of four and three respectively, they replace the former scores. On Wednesday of the second week, however, Kim only made three of the attempted free throws. Because this is lower than the total of six that Kim made the Wednesday before, it is not recorded.

	M	T	W	Th	F
Kim	4 5	3 6	6	5 4	4
Chris	5	4 5	5 4	7 4	5

This type of activity can be open-ended. If participants are consistently hitting ten shots, for example, they can continue to see how far they can go without missing.

VARIATIONS: Let's Improve can be implemented with a wide array of activities. Some which readily come to mind are activities such as kicking soccer goals, serving a volleyball, and throwing a softball for distance or accuracy.

SPECIAL SKILLS NEEDED FOR PARTICIPATION: Dependent upon the activity area selected.

GROUP SIZE: Works best when group members are paired up, but can be used with groups of all sizes.

AGE GROUP: Eight to 12 years.

NUMBER OF FACILITATORS: One facilitator per group of 20 is usually sufficient.

DESCRIPTION OF EQUIPMENT AND FACILITIES: Dependent upon the activity.

TIME REQUIREMENT: This is an ongoing type of activity that can be conducted for the duration of a week, two weeks, or even a month. It's important to keep enthusiasm high. If the facilitator sees that participants have either reached a plateau in regards to skill development or are starting to become a little apathetic in terms of participation, it's time to go on to something else.

ACTIVITY TITLE: Bucket Brigade

GENERAL DESCRIPTION AND OBJECTIVE(S): This is a simple relay activity that incorporates cooperation and social interaction with physical involvement. By the end of Bucket Brigade, participants should be breathing a little harder, have their hearts pumping a little faster, and perhaps have their clothing a little wetter.

Divide the participants into several teams, each team having a water bucket and two large garbage cans, water barrels, or wash tubs. One water barrel should be filled with water and located approximately 50 or so yards away from the team members. The remaining barrel should be empty and placed in front of the relay team. The objective is for each team member to take the team water bucket, run to his/her respective full barrel of water, fill the bucket, run back, and empty the bucket into the other barrel. The water bucket is then passed to the next participant and the relay continues.

Participants continue carrying water until one team fills its barrel.

VARIATIONS: The variations are limited only by the facilitator's imagination. One variation, in case it is found that the groups' interest level is still high, is to then reverse the procedure and fill the original full barrels with the contents from the original empty barrels. Usually by this time participants are pretty well tired out and are willing to slow things down a bit by helping to clean up the activity area.

Another variation is to incorporate this activity with the Build a Fire activity, in order to ensure that all fires are put dead out.

SPECIAL SKILLS NEEDED FOR PARTICIPATION: None.

GROUP SIZE: The group can vary in size for this activity, but it's nice to have at least two teams with four to six participants on each team. If it's part of the facilitator's objective to give the participants a good workout, the teams can be reduced in size in order to increase the amount of activity for each participant. With several teams of only three or four participants per team, competition, as well as aerobic activity, can becme fairly intense.

AGE GROUP: Eight and older. Note: This activity is really a barrel of fun (excuse the pun) for all ages, but usually children under eight years of age have a little difficulty lugging a three-gallon bucket full of water over any measurable distance.

NUMBER OF FACILITATORS: While one facilitator can handle this activity, two are usually better. One facilitator usually stands by the barrels of water while the other facilitator is positioned by the teams and the empty barrels.

DESCRIPTION OF EQUIPMENT AND FACILITIES: There should be two water barrels for

each team. These can be large galvanized wash tubs, garbage cans, old oil drums, etc. In addition, each team should have a water bucket for transporting water from one barrel to the other. A three-gallon bucket is usually about right, although a one-gallon bucket can be used. A smaller bucket, however, means more trips, which might become a little boring after awhile.

A large level field is a good area for this activity. A 50-yard run each way for the participants is a pretty good distance when one is carrying 10 to 20 pounds of water. Facilitators have the option, of course, to either shorten or lengthen the distance, depending upon participants, interest level, and objectives of the activity.

SAFETY AND ENVIRONMENTAL CONSIDERATIONS: This can be an environmental concern in an area where there are obvious drought conditions. No matter how careful one tries to be, water is inevitably sloshed all over the place.

TIME REQUIREMENT: It is surprising how fast this activity can go once you get started. Usually 30 minutes is plenty of time.

64